Inspire

Psalms

NLT

Tyndale House Publishers, Inc.
Carol Stream, Illinois

Published by Christian Art Publishers, PO Box 1599, Vereeniging, 1930, RSA.

Distributed by Tyndale House Publishers, Inc.

Extrabiblical artwork, cover design, and product design copyright © 2016 by Christian Art Publishers.

Images used under license from Shutterstock.com. All rights reserved.

Illustrations by Annabelle Grobler

ISBN 978-1-4964-1987-3 Softcover

Printed in China

22	21	20	19	18	17	16
7	6	5	4	3	2	1

This is the DAY the Lord has made. We will REJOICE and be GLAD in it — Psalm 118:24

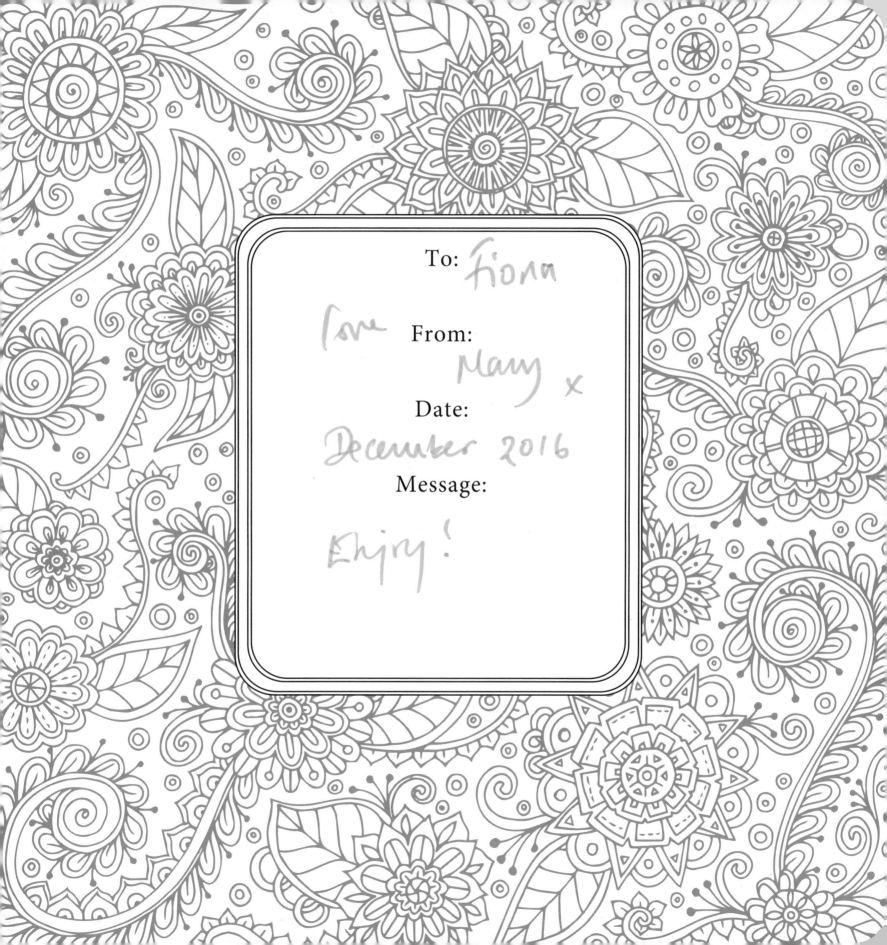

To: Fiona

Love

From:

Mary x

Date:

December 2016

Message:

Enjoy!

I will Guide you along the BEST pathway for your LIFE

Psalm 32:8

Welcome to Inspire: Psalms!

The book of Psalms is filled with heartfelt praise and worship—as well as prayers of joy, heartache, and despair. *Inspire: Psalms* offers creative space right alongside the biblical text for you to interact with Scripture in a unique, life-giving, hope-filled, and healing way— wherever you are in your faith journey! Scripture is God's inspired Word, and it leads us to a better understanding of him. It also teaches us about our identity and reveals God's intended purpose for our lives. It is fresh and relevant and powerful! Time spent in God's Word is time spent with God—and Bible journaling is breathing all-new life into Scripture reading.

Lingering in God's Word through coloring and art journaling not only plants his inspired words more deeply in our hearts and draws us closer to God; it also makes it easier to remember Scripture because we've made it personal through our art on the page. The process of coloring and art journaling engages our imaginations and invites us to reflect on Scripture as we envision how to express the key truths a passage teaches us about God. Our worshipful coloring and creative journaling reflects our faith journey and becomes a personal expression of God's movement in our lives. It is an expressive, artistic way of studying God's Word where the art becomes a reminder of how we are growing in our faith journey. When we journal in this way, we are creating a visual representation of what God is writing on our heart through his Word. It becomes a way to remember and share with others what God is teaching us.

If you are new to Bible journaling, you may find this process helpful:

Pray

Ask the Holy Spirit to be present in your time in God's Word.

Read

Read a portion of Scripture.

Ask

What stands out in this passage?
What does this passage say about God?
How does this passage inform how I live?

Respond

Use the margins to create an image as a response to what you learned through these three questions:
    What images come to mind?
    What phrase or verse will you highlight?
    What colors come to mind?

There is no wrong way to be creative with your application of God's Word. So grab your favorite tools and get started!

May God bless you richly as you linger in the Psalms and create a beautiful collection of your praise and worship on the pages of this book. It is sure to become a spiritual heirloom you will treasure for many years to come!

I will Sing of the Lord's unfailing love forever

Psalm 89:1

PSALMS

BOOK ONE (Psalms 1–41)

1 ¹ Oh, the joys of those who do not
        follow the advice of the wicked,
    or stand around with sinners,
        or join in with mockers.

² But they *delight* in the law of the LORD,
        meditating on it *day & night.*

³ They are like trees planted along the riverbank,
        bearing fruit each season.
    Their leaves never wither,
        and they prosper in all they do.

⁴ But not the wicked!
        They are like worthless chaff, scattered by the wind.
⁵ They will be condemned at the time of judgment.
        Sinners will have no place among the godly.

⁶ For the *Lord* watches
over the path of the *godly,*
    but the path of the wicked
        leads to destruction.

2 ¹ Why are the nations so angry?
        Why do they waste their time with futile plans?
² The kings of the earth prepare for battle;
        the rulers plot together
    against the LORD
        and against his anointed one.
³ "Let us break their chains," they cry,
        "and free ourselves from slavery to God."

⁴ But the one who rules in heaven laughs.
        The Lord scoffs at them.
⁵ Then in anger he rebukes them,
        terrifying them with his fierce fury.
⁶ For the Lord declares, "I have placed my chosen king on the throne
        in Jerusalem, on my holy mountain."

Serve the LORD with reverent FEAR

Psalm 2:11

7 The king proclaims the LORD's decree:
  "The LORD said to me, 'You are my son.
    Today I have become your Father.
8 Only ask, and I will give you the nations as your inheritance,
    the whole earth as your possession.
9 You will break them with an iron rod
    and smash them like clay pots.'"

10 Now then, you kings, act wisely!
    Be warned, you rulers of the earth!
11 *Serve the Lord with reverent fear,*
   & rejoice with trembling.

12 Submit to God's royal son, or he will become angry,
    and you will be destroyed in the midst of all your
      activities—
  for his anger flares up in an instant.
    But what joy for all who take refuge in him!

3 *A psalm of David, regarding the time David fled from his son Absalom.*

1 O LORD, I have so many enemies;
    so many are against me.
2 So many are saying,
  "God will never rescue him!"   *Interlude*

3 But you, O LORD, are a shield around me;
    you are my glory, the one who holds my head high.
4 I cried out to the LORD,
    and he answered me from his holy mountain.   *Interlude*

5 *I lay down and slept,*
    yet I woke up in safety,
  for the Lord was watching
                    over me.
6 I am not afraid of ten thousand enemies
    who surround me on every side.

7 Arise, O LORD!
    Rescue me, my God!
  Slap all my enemies in the face!
    Shatter the teeth of the wicked!
8 Victory comes from you, O LORD.
    May you bless your people.   *Interlude*

4 *For the choir director: A psalm of David, to be accompanied by stringed instruments.*

¹ Answer me when I call to you,
   O God who declares me innocent.
   Free me from my troubles.
   Have mercy on me and hear my prayer.

² How long will you people ruin my reputation?
   How long will you make groundless accusations?
   How long will you continue your lies?   *Interlude*

³ You can be *sure of this:*
   The Lord set apart the *godly* for himself.

   The Lord will answer when I call to him.

⁴ Don't sin by letting anger control you.
   Think about it overnight and remain silent.   *Interlude*
⁵ Offer sacrifices in the right spirit,
   and trust the Lord.

⁶ Many people say, "Who will show us better times?"
   Let your face smile on us, Lord.
⁷ You have given me greater joy
   than those who have abundant harvests of grain and new wine.

⁸ In *peace* I will lie down *& sleep,*
       for you alone,
   O Lord, will keep me *safe.*

5 *For the choir director: A psalm of David, to be accompanied by the flute.*

¹ O Lord, hear me as I pray;
   pay attention to my groaning.
² Listen to my cry for help, my King and my God,
   for I pray to no one but you.
³ Listen to my voice in the morning, Lord.
   Each morning I bring my requests to you and wait expectantly.

⁴ O God, you take no pleasure in wickedness;
   you cannot tolerate the sins of the wicked.
⁵ Therefore, the proud may not stand in your presence,
   for you hate all who do evil.
⁶ You will destroy those who tell lies.
   The Lord detests murderers and deceivers.

⁷ Because of your unfailing love, I can enter your house;
   I will worship at your Temple with deepest awe.

Psalm 5:8

8 *Lead me* in the right path, *O Lord,*
or my enemies will conquer me.
Make your way plain for me to *follow.*

9 My enemies cannot speak a truthful word.
Their deepest desire is to destroy others.
Their talk is foul, like the stench from an open grave.
Their tongues are filled with flattery.
10 O God, declare them guilty.
Let them be caught in their own traps.
Drive them away because of their many sins,
for they have rebelled against you.

11 But let all who take refuge in you rejoice;
let them sing joyful praises forever.
Spread your protection over them,
that all who love your name may be filled with joy.
12 For you bless the godly, O Lord;
you surround them with your shield of love.

6 *For the choir director: A psalm of David, to be accompanied by an eight-stringed instrument.*

1 O Lord, don't rebuke me in your anger
or discipline me in your rage.
2 Have compassion on me, Lord, for I am weak.
Heal me, Lord, for my bones are in agony.
3 I am sick at heart.
How long, O Lord, until you restore me?

4 Return, O Lord, and rescue me.
Save me because of your unfailing love.
5 For the dead do not remember you.
Who can praise you from the grave?

6 I am worn out from sobbing.
All night I flood my bed with weeping,
drenching it with my tears.
7 My vision is blurred by grief;
my eyes are worn out because of all my enemies.

8 *Go away,* all you who do evil, for the *Lord* has heard my weeping. **9** *The Lord* has heard my plea;
the *Lord* will answer *my prayer.*

10 May all my enemies be disgraced and terrified.
May they suddenly turn back in shame.

7 *A psalm of David, which he sang to the LORD concerning Cush of the tribe of Benjamin.*

¹ I come to you for protection, O LORD my God.
　　Save me from my persecutors—rescue me!
² If you don't, they will maul me like a lion,
　　tearing me to pieces with no one to rescue me.
³ O LORD my God, if I have done wrong
　　or am guilty of injustice,
⁴ if I have betrayed a friend
　　or plundered my enemy without cause,
⁵ then let my enemies capture me.
　　Let them trample me into the ground
　　and drag my honor in the dust. *Interlude*

⁶ Arise, O LORD, in anger!
　　Stand up against the fury of my enemies!
　　Wake up, my God, and bring justice!
⁷ Gather the nations before you.
　　Rule over them from on high.
⁸ 　The LORD judges the nations.
　Declare me righteous, O LORD,
　　for I am innocent, O Most High!
⁹ End the evil of those who are wicked,
　　and defend the righteous.
　For you look deep within the mind and heart,
　　O righteous God.

¹⁰ *God is my shield,*
saving those whose hearts
are true & right.

¹¹ God is an honest judge.
　　He is angry with the wicked every day.

¹² If a person does not repent,
　　God will sharpen his sword;
　　he will bend and string his bow.
¹³ He will prepare his deadly weapons
　　and shoot his flaming arrows.

¹⁴ The wicked conceive evil;
　　they are pregnant with trouble
　　and give birth to lies.
¹⁵ They dig a deep pit to trap others,
　　then fall into it themselves.
¹⁶ The trouble they make for others backfires on them.
　　The violence they plan falls on their own heads.

¹⁷ I will thank the LORD because he is just;
　　I will sing praise to the name of the LORD Most High.

Your Glory is HIGHER THAN THE HEAVENS

Psalm 8:1

8 *For the choir director: A psalm of David, to be accompanied by a stringed instrument.*

¹ O Lord, our Lord,
your majestic name
fills the earth!
Your glory is higher than the heavens.
² You have taught children and infants
to tell of your strength,
silencing your enemies
and all who oppose you.

³ When I look at the night sky &
see the work of
your fingers —
the moon and the stars you set in place —
⁴ what are mere mortals that you should think about them,
human beings that you should care for them?
⁵ Yet you made them only a little lower than God
and crowned them with glory and honor.
⁶ You gave them charge of everything you made,
putting all things under their authority—
⁷ the flocks and the herds
and all the wild animals,
⁸ the birds in the sky, the fish in the sea,
and everything that swims the ocean currents.

⁹ O Lord, our Lord, your majestic name fills the earth!

9 *For the choir director: A psalm of David, to be sung to the tune "Death of the Son."*

¹ I will praise you, Lord,
with all my heart; I will tell of
all the marvelous things you have done.
² I will be filled with joy because of you.
I will sing praises to your name, O Most High.

³ My enemies retreated;
they staggered and died when you appeared.
⁴ For you have judged in my favor;
from your throne you have judged with fairness.
⁵ You have rebuked the nations and destroyed the wicked;
you have erased their names forever.
⁶ The enemy is finished, in endless ruins;
the cities you uprooted are now forgotten.

⁷ But the LORD reigns forever,
    executing judgment from his throne.
⁸ He will judge the world with justice
    and rule the nations with fairness.

⁹ *The Lord* is a *shelter*

for the oppressed, a *refuge* in times of trouble.

¹⁰ Those who know your name trust in you,
    for you, O LORD, do not abandon those who search
      for you.

¹¹ Sing praises to the LORD who reigns in Jerusalem.
    Tell the world about his unforgettable deeds.
¹² For he who avenges murder cares for the helpless.
    He does not ignore the cries of those who suffer.

¹³ LORD, have mercy on me.
    See how my enemies torment me.
    Snatch me back from the jaws of death.
¹⁴ Save me so I can praise you publicly at Jerusalem's gates,
    so I can rejoice that you have rescued me.

¹⁵ The nations have fallen into the pit they dug for others.
    Their own feet have been caught in the trap they set.
¹⁶ The LORD is known for his justice.
    The wicked are trapped by their own deeds.   *Quiet Interlude*

¹⁷ The wicked will go down to the grave.
    This is the fate of all the nations who ignore God.

¹⁸ But the *needy*
will not be ignored forever; the *hopes*

of the poor will not always be crushed.

¹⁹ Arise, O LORD!
    Do not let mere mortals defy you!
    Judge the nations!
²⁰ Make them tremble in fear, O LORD.
    Let the nations know they are merely human.   *Interlude*

10 ¹ O LORD, why do you stand so far away?
    Why do you hide when I am in trouble?
² The wicked arrogantly hunt down the poor.
    Let them be caught in the evil they plan for others.
³ For they brag about their evil desires;
    they praise the greedy and curse the LORD.

⁴ The wicked are too proud to seek God.
    They seem to think that God is dead.
⁵ Yet they succeed in everything they do.
    They do not see your punishment awaiting them.
    They sneer at all their enemies.

6 They think, "Nothing bad will ever happen to us!
    We will be free of trouble forever!"

7 Their mouths are full of cursing, lies, and threats.
    Trouble and evil are on the tips of their tongues.
8 They lurk in ambush in the villages,
    waiting to murder innocent people.
    They are always searching for helpless victims.
9 Like lions crouched in hiding,
    they wait to pounce on the helpless.
  Like hunters they capture the helpless
    and drag them away in nets.
10 Their helpless victims are crushed;
    they fall beneath the strength of the wicked.
11 The wicked think, "God isn't watching us!
    He has closed his eyes and won't even see what we do!"

12 Arise, O Lord!
    Punish the wicked, O God!
    Do not ignore the helpless!
13 Why do the wicked get away with despising God?
    They think, "God will never call us to account."
14 But you see the trouble and grief they cause.
    You take note of it and punish them.
  The helpless put their trust in you.
    You defend the orphans.

15 Break the arms of these wicked, evil people!
    Go after them until the last one is destroyed.
16 The Lord is king forever and ever!
    The godless nations will vanish from the land.
17 *Lord, you know the hopes
    of the helpless. Surely you will
        hear their cries and comfort them.*

18 You will bring justice to the orphans and the oppressed,
    so mere people can no longer terrify them.

11 *For the choir director: A psalm of David.*

1 *I trust in the Lord
        for protection.*

  So why do you say to me,
    "Fly like a bird to the mountains for safety!
2 The wicked are stringing their bows
    and fitting their arrows on the bowstrings.
  They shoot from the shadows
    at those whose hearts are right.

³ The foundations of law and order have
    collapsed.
      What can the righteous do?"

⁴But the LORD is in his **holy Temple;** the LORD
still rules from *heaven.* He watches everyone
closely, examining every person on *earth.*

⁵ The LORD examines both the righteous and the wicked.
    He hates those who love violence.
⁶ He will rain down blazing coals and burning sulfur on the wicked,
    punishing them with scorching winds.

⁷For the
righteous Lord loves justice.
    The virtuous will see his face.

12 *For the choir director: A psalm of David, to be accompanied by an eight-stringed instrument.*

¹ Help, O LORD, for the godly are fast disappearing!
    The faithful have vanished from the earth!
² Neighbors lie to each other,
    speaking with flattering lips and deceitful hearts.
³ May the LORD cut off their flattering lips
    and silence their boastful tongues.
⁴ They say, "We will lie to our hearts' content.
    Our lips are our own—who can stop us?"

⁵ The LORD replies, "I have seen violence done to the helpless,
    and I have heard the groans of the poor.
Now I will rise up to rescue them,
    as they have longed for me to do."

⁶ *The Lord's promises* are *pure,*
like *silver* refined in a furnace,
    purified seven times over.

⁷ Therefore, LORD, we know you will protect the oppressed,
    preserving them forever from this lying generation,
⁸ even though the wicked strut about,
    and evil is praised throughout the land.

13 *For the choir director: A psalm of David.*

¹ O LORD, how long will you forget me? Forever?
    How long will you look the other way?
² How long must I struggle with anguish in my soul,
    with sorrow in my heart every day?
      How long will my enemy have the upper hand?

The LORD'S PROMISES are PURE, like Silver

Psalm 12:6

BUT I trust in Your unfailing Love
Psalm 13:5

³ Turn and answer me, O LORD my God!
   Restore the sparkle to my eyes, or I will die.
⁴ Don't let my enemies gloat, saying, "We have defeated him!"
   Don't let them rejoice at my downfall.

⁵ But I *trust* in your unfailing *love.*
   I will *rejoice* because you have
                    rescued me.
⁶ I will *sing* to the *Lord*
            because he is *good* to me.

14 *For the choir director: A psalm of David.*

¹ Only fools say in their hearts,
   "There is no God."
They are corrupt, and their actions are evil;
   not one of them does good!

² The LORD looks down from heaven
   on the entire human race;
he looks to see if anyone is truly wise,
   if anyone seeks God.
³ But no, all have turned away;
   all have become corrupt.
No one does good,
   not a single one!

⁴ Will those who do evil never learn?
   They eat up my people like bread
   and wouldn't think of praying to the LORD.
⁵ Terror will grip them,
   for God is with those who obey him.
⁶ The wicked frustrate the plans of the oppressed,
   but the LORD will protect his people.

⁷ Who will come from Mount Zion to rescue Israel?
   When the LORD restores his people,
   Jacob will shout with joy, and Israel will rejoice.

15 *A psalm of David.*

¹ Who may *worship* in your
         sanctuary, Lord?

Who may enter your presence on your holy hill?
² Those who lead blameless lives and do what is right,
   speaking the truth from sincere hearts.

³ Those who refuse to gossip
   or harm their neighbors
   or speak evil of their friends.
⁴ Those who despise flagrant sinners,
   and honor the faithful followers of the LORD,
   and keep their promises even when it hurts.
⁵ Those who lend money without charging interest,
   and who cannot be bribed to lie about the innocent.
  Such people will stand firm forever.

16 *A psalm of David.*

¹ *Keep me safe, O God,*
  for I have come to you for *refuge.*

² I said to the LORD, "You are my Master!
   Every good thing I have comes from you."
³ The godly people in the land
   are my true heroes!
   I take pleasure in them!
⁴ Troubles multiply for those who chase after other gods.
   I will not take part in their sacrifices of blood
   or even speak the names of their gods.

⁵ *Lord,* you alone are my
  inheritance, my cup of *blessing.*
   You guard all that is mine.
⁶ The land you have given me is a pleasant land.
   What a wonderful inheritance!

⁷ I will bless the LORD who guides me;
   even at night my heart instructs me.
⁸ I know the LORD is always with me.
   I will not be shaken, for he is right beside me.

⁹ No wonder my heart is glad, and I rejoice.
   My body rests in safety.
¹⁰ For you will not leave my soul among the dead
   or allow your holy one to rot in the grave.

¹¹ *You will show me the way of life,* granting me
  the *joy* of your presence and the pleasures
   of living with you *forever.*

KEEP ME SAFE, O God, I have come to you for REFUGE.

Psalm 16:1

17 *A prayer of David.*

¹ O Lᴏʀᴅ, hear my plea for justice.
 Listen to my cry for help.
 Pay attention to my prayer,
 for it comes from honest lips.
² Declare me innocent,
 for you see those who do right.

³ *You have tested my thoughts* and examined my
heart in the night. You have scrutinized
me and found nothing wrong. I am determined
 not to sin in what I say.
⁴ I have followed your commands,
 which keep me from following cruel and evil people.
⁵ My steps have stayed on your path;
 I have not wavered from following you.

⁶ I am praying to you because I know you will answer, O God.
 Bend down and listen as I pray.
⁷ Show me your unfailing love in wonderful ways.
 By your mighty power you rescue
 those who seek refuge from their enemies.

⁸ *Guard me*
as you would guard your *own eyes.*
Hide me in the shadow *of your wings.*

⁹ Protect me from wicked people who attack me,
 from murderous enemies who surround me.
¹⁰ They are without pity.
 Listen to their boasting!
¹¹ They track me down and surround me,
 watching for the chance to throw me to the ground.
¹² They are like hungry lions, eager to tear me apart—
 like young lions hiding in ambush.

¹³ Arise, O Lᴏʀᴅ!
 Stand against them, and bring them to their knees!
 Rescue me from the wicked with your sword!
¹⁴ By the power of your hand, O Lᴏʀᴅ,
 destroy those who look to this world for their reward.
 But satisfy the hunger of your treasured ones.
 May their children have plenty,
 leaving an inheritance for their descendants.
¹⁵ Because I am righteous, I will see you.
 When I awake, I will see you face to face and be satisfied.

THE *Lord* is my ROCK, my FORTRESS, AND MY *Savior*

Psalm 18:2

18 *For the choir director: A psalm of David, the servant of the LORD. He sang this song to the LORD on the day the LORD rescued him from all his enemies and from Saul. He sang:*

¹ I love you, LORD;
  you are my strength.
   ² *The LORD is my rock, my fortress, and my*
   savior; my God is my rock, in whom
I find *protection. He is my shield, the power that*
   saves me, and my place of safety.

³ I called on the LORD, who is worthy of praise,
  and he saved me from my enemies.

⁴ The ropes of death entangled me;
  floods of destruction swept over me.
⁵ The grave wrapped its ropes around me;
  death laid a trap in my path.
⁶ But in my distress I cried out to the LORD;
  yes, I prayed to my God for help.
  He heard me from his sanctuary;
  my cry to him reached his ears.

⁷ Then the earth quaked and trembled.
  The foundations of the mountains shook;
  they quaked because of his anger.
⁸ Smoke poured from his nostrils;
  fierce flames leaped from his mouth.
  Glowing coals blazed forth from him.
⁹ He opened the heavens and came down;
  dark storm clouds were beneath his feet.
¹⁰ Mounted on a mighty angelic being, he flew,
  soaring on the wings of the wind.
¹¹ He shrouded himself in darkness,
  veiling his approach with dark rain clouds.
¹² Thick clouds shielded the brightness around him
  and rained down hail and burning coals.
¹³ The LORD thundered from heaven;
  the voice of the Most High resounded
  amid the hail and burning coals.
¹⁴ He shot his arrows and scattered his enemies;
  great bolts of lightning flashed, and they were confused.
¹⁵ Then at your command, O LORD,
  at the blast of your breath,
  the bottom of the sea could be seen,
  and the foundations of the earth were laid bare.

¹⁶ *He reached down from heaven*
  and rescued me; he drew me
  out of deep waters.

¹⁷ He rescued me from my powerful enemies,
    from those who hated me and were too strong for me.
¹⁸ They attacked me at a moment when I was in distress,
    but the LORD supported me.
¹⁹ *He led me to a place of safety;*
    he rescued me
      because he delights in me.

²⁰ The LORD rewarded me for doing right;
    he restored me because of my innocence.
²¹ For I have kept the ways of the LORD;
    I have not turned from my God to follow evil.
²² I have followed all his regulations;
    I have never abandoned his decrees.
²³ I am blameless before God;
    I have kept myself from sin.
²⁴ The LORD rewarded me for doing right.
    He has seen my innocence.

²⁵ *To the faithful you show yourself faithful;*

    to those with integrity you show integrity.
²⁶ To the pure you show yourself pure,
    but to the crooked you show yourself shrewd.
²⁷ You rescue the humble,
    but you humiliate the proud.
²⁸ You light a lamp for me.
    The LORD, my God, lights up my darkness.
²⁹ In your strength I can crush an army;
    with my God I can scale any wall.

³⁰ God's way is perfect.
    All the LORD's promises prove true.
    He is a shield for all who look to him for protection.
³¹ For who is God except the LORD?
    Who but our God is a solid rock?
³² God arms me with strength,
    and he makes my way perfect.
³³ He makes me as surefooted as a deer,
    enabling me to stand on mountain heights.
³⁴ He trains my hands for battle;
    he strengthens my arm to draw a bronze bow.
³⁵ You have given me your shield of victory.
    Your right hand supports me;
    your help has made me great.
³⁶ You have made a wide path for my feet
    to keep them from slipping.

³⁷ I chased my enemies and caught them;
    I did not stop until they were conquered.
³⁸ I struck them down so they could not get up;
    they fell beneath my feet.

39 You have armed me with *strength*
for the battle; you have subdued
my enemies *under my feet.*

40 You placed my foot on their necks.
I have destroyed all who hated me.
41 They called for help, but no one came to their rescue.
They even cried to the LORD, but he refused to answer.
42 I ground them as fine as dust in the wind.
I swept them into the gutter like dirt.
43 You gave me victory over my accusers.
You appointed me ruler over nations;
people I don't even know now serve me.
44 As soon as they hear of me, they submit;
foreign nations cringe before me.
45 They all lose their courage
and come trembling from their strongholds.

46 *The Lord lives!* *Praise* to my Rock!
May the God of my *salvation* be exalted!

47 He is the God who pays back those who harm me;
he subdues the nations under me
48 and rescues me from my enemies.
You hold me safe beyond the reach of my enemies;
you save me from violent opponents.
49 For this, O LORD, I will praise you among the nations;
I will sing praises to your name.
50 You give great victories to your king;
you show unfailing love to your anointed,
to David and all his descendants forever.

19 *For the choir director: A psalm of David.*

1 The heavens proclaim the glory of God.
The skies display his craftsmanship.
2 Day after day they continue to speak;
night after night they make him known.
3 They speak without a sound or word;
their voice is never heard.
4 Yet their message has gone throughout the earth,
and their words to all the world.

God has made a home in the heavens for the sun.
5 It bursts forth like a radiant bridegroom after his wedding.
It rejoices like a great athlete eager to run the race.
6 The sun rises at one end of the heavens
and follows its course to the other end.
Nothing can hide from its heat.

⁷*The instructions of the Lord are perfect,*
reviving the soul. The decrees of the LORD are
trustworthy, making wise the simple.

⁸ The commandments of the LORD are right,
  bringing joy to the heart.
The commands of the LORD are clear,
  giving insight for living.
⁹ Reverence for the LORD is pure,
  lasting forever.
The laws of the LORD are true;
  each one is fair.
¹⁰ They are more desirable than gold,
  even the finest gold.
They are sweeter than honey,
  even honey dripping from the comb.
¹¹ They are a warning to your servant,
  a great reward for those who obey them.

¹² How can I know all the sins lurking in my heart?
  Cleanse me from these hidden faults.
¹³ Keep your servant from deliberate sins!
  Don't let them control me.
Then I will be free of guilt
  and innocent of great sin.

¹⁴ May the words of my mouth
  and the meditation of my heart
be pleasing to you,
  O LORD, my rock and my redeemer.

20 *For the choir director: A psalm of David.*

¹ In times of trouble, may the LORD answer your cry.
  May the name of the God of Jacob keep you safe from
    all harm.
² May he send you help from his sanctuary
  and strengthen you from Jerusalem.
³ May he remember all your gifts
  and look favorably on your burnt offerings.

⁴*May he
grant your heart's desires
and make all your plans succeed.*

Interlude

⁵ May we shout for joy when we hear of your victory
  and raise a victory banner in the name of our God.
May the LORD answer all your prayers.

⁶ Now I know that the LORD rescues his anointed king.
  He will answer him from his holy heaven
    and rescue him by his great power.

MAY He grant your Heart's Desires and make all your PLANS SUCCEED

Psalm 20:4

With Music and Singing we Celebrate Your Mighty Acts

PSALM 21:13

7 Some nations boast of their chariots and horses,
  but we boast in the name of the Lord our God.
8 Those nations will fall down and collapse,
  but we will rise up and stand firm.

9 *Give victory* to our *king, O Lord!*
  Answer our cry for help.

21 *For the choir director: A psalm of David.*

1 How the king rejoices in your strength, O Lord!
  He shouts with joy because you give him victory.
2 For you have given him his heart's desire;
  you have withheld nothing he requested. *Interlude*

3 You welcomed him back with success and prosperity.
  You placed a crown of finest gold on his head.
4 He asked you to preserve his life,
  and you granted his request.
  The days of his life stretch on forever.
5 Your victory brings him great honor,
  and you have clothed him with splendor and majesty.
6 You have endowed him with eternal blessings
  and given him the joy of your presence.
7 For the king trusts in the Lord.

The *unfailing love* of the
  Most High will keep him from stumbling.

8 You will capture all your enemies.
  Your strong right hand will seize all who hate you.
9 You will throw them in a flaming furnace
  when you appear.
The Lord will consume them in his anger;
  fire will devour them.
10 You will wipe their children from the face of the earth;
  they will never have descendants.
11 Although they plot against you,
  their evil schemes will never succeed.
12 For they will turn and run
  when they see your arrows aimed at them.

13 *Rise up, O Lord, in all your power.*
  With music and singing we celebrate
  your mighty acts.

22 *For the choir director: A psalm of David, to be sung to the tune "Doe of the Dawn."*

¹ My God, my God, why have you abandoned me?
  Why are you so far away when I groan for help?
² Every day I call to you, my God, but you do not answer.
  Every night I lift my voice, but I find no relief.

³ Yet you are holy,
  enthroned on the praises of Israel.
⁴ Our ancestors trusted in you,
  and you rescued them.
⁵ They cried out to you and were saved.
  They trusted in you and were never disgraced.

⁶ But I am a worm and not a man.
  I am scorned and despised by all!
⁷ Everyone who sees me mocks me.
  They sneer and shake their heads, saying,
⁸ "Is this the one who relies on the LORD?
  Then let the LORD save him!
 If the LORD loves him so much,
  let the LORD rescue him!"

⁹ Yet you brought me safely from my mother's womb
  and led me to trust you at my mother's breast.
¹⁰ I was thrust into your arms at my birth.

You have been my God LORD from the moment I was born.

¹¹ Do not stay so far from me,
  for trouble is near,
  and no one else can help me.
¹² My enemies surround me like a herd of bulls;
  fierce bulls of Bashan have hemmed me in!
¹³ Like lions they open their jaws against me,
  roaring and tearing into their prey.
¹⁴ My life is poured out like water,
  and all my bones are out of joint.
 My heart is like wax,
  melting within me.
¹⁵ My strength has dried up like sunbaked clay.
  My tongue sticks to the roof of my mouth.
  You have laid me in the dust and left me for dead.
¹⁶ My enemies surround me like a pack of dogs;
  an evil gang closes in on me.
  They have pierced my hands and feet.
¹⁷ I can count all my bones.
  My enemies stare at me and gloat.
¹⁸ They divide my garments among themselves
  and throw dice for my clothing.

The LORD is my Shepherd, I have all that I need

Psalm 23:1

19 O Lord, do not stay far away!
You are my strength;
come quickly to my aid!
20 Save me from the sword;
spare my precious life from these dogs.
21 Snatch me from the lion's jaws
and from the horns of these wild oxen.

22 I will proclaim your name to my brothers and sisters.
I will praise you among your assembled people.
23 Praise the LORD, all you who fear him!
Honor him, all you descendants of Jacob!
Show him reverence, all you descendants of Israel!
24 For he has not ignored or belittled the suffering of the needy.
He has not turned his back on them,
but has listened to their cries for help.

25 I will praise you in the great assembly.
I will fulfill my vows in the presence of those who
worship you.
26 The poor will eat and be satisfied.
All who seek the LORD will praise him.
Their hearts will rejoice with everlasting joy.
27 The whole earth will acknowledge the LORD and return to him.
All the families of the nations will bow down before him.

28 *For royal power belongs to the Lord.*
He rules all the nations.

29 Let the rich of the earth feast and worship.
Bow before him, all who are mortal,
all whose lives will end as dust.
30 Our children will also serve him.
Future generations will hear about the wonders of the Lord.
31 His righteous acts will be told to those not yet born.
They will hear about everything he has done.

23 *A psalm of David.*

1 The LORD is my shepherd;
I have all that I need.
2 He lets me rest in green meadows;
he leads me beside peaceful streams.
3 He renews my strength.
He guides me along right paths,
bringing honor to his name.

⁴ Even when I walk
   through the darkest valley,
 I will not be afraid,
    for you are close beside me.
 Your rod and your staff
    protect and comfort me.
⁵ You prepare a feast for me
    in the presence of my enemies.
 You honor me by anointing my head with oil.
    My cup overflows with blessings.
⁶ Surely your goodness and unfailing love will pursue me
    all the days of my life,
 and I will live in the house of the LORD
    forever.

24 *A psalm of David.*

¹*The earth is the* Lord's,
    *and everything in it. The world and all
       its people* belong to him.

² For he laid the earth's foundation on the seas
    and built it on the ocean depths.

³ Who may climb the mountain of the LORD?
    Who may stand in his holy place?
⁴ Only those whose hands and hearts are pure,
    who do not worship idols
    and never tell lies.
⁵ They will receive the LORD's blessing
    and have a right relationship with God their savior.
⁶ Such people may seek you
    and worship in your presence, O God of Jacob.   *Interlude*

⁷ Open up, ancient gates!
    Open up, ancient doors,
    and let the King of glory enter.

⁸*Who is the* King of glory? *The* Lord,
    strong and mighty,
    the Lord, *invincible in battle.*
⁹ Open up, ancient gates!
    Open up, ancient doors,
    and let the King of glory enter.
¹⁰ Who is the King of glory?
    The LORD of Heaven's Armies—
    he is the King of glory.   *Interlude*

25 *A psalm of David.*

[1] O LORD, I give my life to you.
[2]   I trust in you, my God!
  Do not let me be disgraced,
    or let my enemies rejoice in my defeat.
[3] No one who trusts in you will ever be disgraced,
    but disgrace comes to those who try to deceive others.

[4] *Show me the right path, O Lord;*
    point out the road for me to follow.

[5] Lead me by your truth and teach me,
    for you are the God who saves me.
    All day long I put my hope in you.
[6] Remember, O LORD, your compassion and unfailing love,
    which you have shown from long ages past.
[7] Do not remember the rebellious sins of my youth.
    Remember me in the light of your unfailing love,
    for you are merciful, O LORD.

[8] The LORD is good and does what is right;
    he shows the proper path to those who go astray.
[9] He leads the humble in doing right,
    teaching them his way.
[10] The LORD leads with unfailing love and faithfulness
    all who keep his covenant and obey his demands.

[11] *For the honor of your name, O Lord;*
    forgive my many, many sins.

[12] Who are those who fear the LORD?
    He will show them the path they should choose.
[13] They will live in prosperity,
    and their children will inherit the land.
[14] The LORD is a friend to those who fear him.
    He teaches them his covenant.
[15] My eyes are always on the LORD,
    for he rescues me from the traps of my enemies.

[16] Turn to me and have mercy,
    for I am alone and in deep distress.
[17] My problems go from bad to worse.
    Oh, save me from them all!
[18] Feel my pain and see my trouble.
    Forgive all my sins.
[19] See how many enemies I have
    and how viciously they hate me!
[20] Protect me! Rescue my life from them!
    Do not let me be disgraced, for in you I take refuge.

25 This psalm is a Hebrew acrostic poem; each verse begins with a successive letter of the Hebrew alphabet.

²¹May *integrity & honesty*
protect me, for I put my *hope* in you.

²² O God, ransom Israel
from all its troubles.

26 *A psalm of David.*

¹ Declare me innocent, O LORD,
for I have acted with integrity;
I have trusted in the LORD without wavering.

²Put me on trial, *Lord*,
and cross-examine me.
Test my motives and my *heart.*

³ For I am always aware of your unfailing love,
and I have lived according to your truth.

⁴ I do not spend time with liars
or go along with hypocrites.

⁵ I hate the gatherings of those who do evil,
and I refuse to join in with the wicked.

⁶ I wash my hands to declare my innocence.
I come to your altar, O LORD,

⁷ singing a song of thanksgiving
and telling of all your wonders.

⁸ I love your sanctuary, *Lord*,
the place where your
glorious presence dwells.

⁹ Don't let me suffer the fate of sinners.
Don't condemn me along with murderers.

¹⁰ Their hands are dirty with evil schemes,
and they constantly take bribes.

¹¹ But I am not like that; I live with integrity.
So redeem me and show me mercy.

¹² Now I stand on solid ground,
and I will publicly praise the LORD.

27 *A psalm of David.*

¹The LORD is my *light* and my *salvation* —
so why should I be afraid? The LORD is my fortress,
protecting me from danger, so why should I tremble?

The *Lord* is my LIGHT AND MY *Salvation*

Psalm 27:1

² When evil people come to devour me,
    when my enemies and foes attack me,
    they will stumble and fall.
³ Though a mighty army surrounds me,
    my heart will not be afraid.
  Even if I am attacked,
    I will remain confident.

⁴ *The one thing* I ask of *the Lord* —
        the thing *I seek most* —
is to live in the house of the LORD all the days of my life,
    delighting in the LORD's perfections
    and meditating in his Temple.
⁵ For he will conceal me there when troubles come;
    he will hide me in his sanctuary.
    He will place me out of reach on a high rock.
⁶ Then I will hold my head high
    above my enemies who surround me.
  At his sanctuary I will offer sacrifices with shouts of joy,
    singing and praising the LORD with music.

⁷ Hear me as I pray, O LORD.
    Be merciful and answer me!
⁸ My heart has heard you say, "Come and talk with me."
    And my heart responds, "LORD, I am coming."
⁹ Do not turn your back on me.
    Do not reject your servant in anger.
    You have always been my helper.
  Don't leave me now; don't abandon me,
    O God of my salvation!
¹⁰ Even if my father and mother abandon me,
    the LORD will hold me close.

¹¹ *Teach me* how to live, *O Lord.*
        Lead me along the *right path,*

    for my enemies are waiting for me.
¹² Do not let me fall into their hands.
    For they accuse me of things I've never done;
    with every breath they threaten me with violence.
¹³ Yet I am confident I will see the LORD's goodness
    while I am here in the land of the living.

¹⁴ Wait *patiently* for the LORD.
    Be brave & courageous.
    Yes, wait patiently for the *Lord.*

THE
LORD IS MY
STRENGTH
✝ AND ✝
SHIELD
I trust him with
ALL MY HEART.

Psalm 28:7

THE LORD is my STRENGTH and SHIELD. I trust HIM with all my Heart

Psalm 28:7

28 *A psalm of David.*

¹ I pray to you, O LORD, my rock.
  Do not turn a deaf ear to me.
For if you are silent,
  I might as well give up and die.
² Listen to my prayer for mercy
  as I cry out to you for help,
  as I lift my hands toward your holy sanctuary.

³ Do not drag me away with the wicked—
  with those who do evil—
those who speak friendly words to their neighbors
  while planning evil in their hearts.
⁴ Give them the punishment they so richly deserve!
  Measure it out in proportion to their wickedness.
Pay them back for all their evil deeds!
  Give them a taste of what they have done to others.
⁵ They care nothing for what the LORD has done
  or for what his hands have made.
So he will tear them down,
  and they will never be rebuilt!

⁶ Praise the LORD!
  For he has heard my cry for mercy.
⁷ The LORD is my *strength and shield*.
    I trust him with all my heart.
    He helps me, and my heart is filled with joy.
    I burst out in songs of thanksgiving.

⁸ The LORD gives his people strength.
  He is a safe fortress for his anointed king.
⁹ Save your people!
  Bless Israel, your special possession.
Lead them like a shepherd,
  and carry them in your arms forever.

29 *A psalm of David.*

¹ *Honor the Lord you heavenly beings;*
honor the LORD for his glory & strength.

² Honor the LORD for the glory of his name.
  Worship the LORD in the splendor of his holiness.

³ The voice of the LORD echoes above the sea.
  The God of glory thunders.
  The LORD thunders over the mighty sea.

4 The voice of the *Lord* is powerful;
   the voice of the Lord is *majestic*.

5 The voice of the Lord splits the mighty cedars;
   the Lord shatters the cedars of Lebanon.
6 He makes Lebanon's mountains skip like a calf;
   he makes Mount Hermon leap like a young wild ox.
7 The voice of the Lord strikes
   with bolts of lightning.
8 The voice of the Lord makes the barren wilderness quake;
   the Lord shakes the wilderness of Kadesh.
9 The voice of the Lord twists mighty oaks
   and strips the forests bare.
  In his Temple everyone shouts, "Glory!"

10 The Lord rules over the floodwaters.
   The Lord reigns as king forever.

11 The Lord *gives his people strength*.
   The Lord *blesses* them with *peace*.

30 *A psalm of David. A song for the dedication of the Temple.*

1 I will exalt you, Lord, for you rescued me.
   You refused to let my enemies triumph over me.
2 O Lord my God, I cried to you for help,
   and you restored my health.
3 You brought me up from the grave, O Lord.
   You kept me from falling into the pit of death.

4 Sing to the Lord, all you godly ones!
   Praise his holy name.
5 For his anger lasts only a moment,
   but his favor lasts a lifetime!
  Weeping may last through the night,
    but joy comes with the morning.

6 When I was prosperous, I said,
   "Nothing can stop me now!"
7 Your favor, O Lord, made me as secure as a mountain.
   Then you turned away from me, and I was shattered.

8 I cried out to you, O Lord.
   I begged the Lord for mercy, saying,
9 "What will you gain if I die,
   if I sink into the grave?
  Can my dust praise you?
   Can it tell of your faithfulness?

RESCUE Me, LORD, for you are a Faithful GOD

PSALM 31:5

¹⁰ Hear me, LORD, and have mercy on me.
Help me, O LORD."

¹¹ You have turned my mourning into joyful dancing.
You have taken away my clothes of mourning and clothed me with joy,
¹² that I might sing praises to you and not be silent.

O Lord my God, I will give you thanks forever!

31 *For the choir director: A psalm of David.*

¹ O LORD, I have come to you for protection;
don't let me be disgraced.
Save me, for you do what is right.
² Turn your ear to listen to me;
rescue me quickly.
Be my rock of protection,
a fortress where I will be safe.
³ You are my rock and my fortress.
For the honor of your name, lead me out of this danger.
⁴ Pull me from the trap my enemies set for me,
for I find protection in you alone.
⁵ I entrust my spirit into your hand.

Rescue me, Lord, for you are a faithful God.

⁶ I hate those who worship worthless idols.
I trust in the LORD.
⁷ I will be glad and rejoice in your unfailing love,
for you have seen my troubles,
and you care about the anguish of my soul.
⁸ You have not handed me over to my enemies
but have set me in a safe place.

⁹ Have mercy on me, LORD, for I am in distress.
Tears blur my eyes.
My body and soul are withering away.
¹⁰ I am dying from grief;
my years are shortened by sadness.
Sin has drained my strength;
I am wasting away from within.
¹¹ I am scorned by all my enemies
and despised by my neighbors—
even my friends are afraid to come near me.
When they see me on the street,
they run the other way.

¹² I am ignored as if I were dead,
     as if I were a broken pot.
¹³ I have heard the many rumors about me,
     and I am surrounded by terror.
   My enemies conspire against me,
     plotting to take my life.

¹⁴ But I am trusting you, O LORD,
     saying, "You are my God!"
¹⁵ *My future is in your hands.*
   Rescue me from those who
     hunt me down relentlessly.
¹⁶ Let your favor shine on your servant.
     In your unfailing love, rescue me.
¹⁷ Don't let me be disgraced, O LORD,
     for I call out to you for help.
   Let the wicked be disgraced;
     let them lie silent in the grave.
¹⁸ Silence their lying lips—
     those proud and arrogant lips that accuse the godly.

¹⁹ *How great* is the *goodness*
     you have stored up for *those* who fear you.
   You lavish it on those who come to you for protection,
     blessing them before the watching world.
²⁰ You hide them in the shelter of your presence,
     safe from those who conspire against them.
   You shelter them in your presence,
     far from accusing tongues.

²¹ Praise the LORD,
     for he has shown me the wonders of his unfailing love.
     He kept me safe when my city was under attack.
²² In panic I cried out,
     "I am cut off from the LORD!"
   But you heard my cry for mercy
     and answered my call for help.

²³ *Love the Lord,* all you godly ones!
   For the LORD protects those who are *loyal* to him,
     but he harshly punishes the arrogant.
²⁴ So be *strong & courageous,*
   all you who put *your hope* in the LORD!

32 *A psalm of David.*

¹ Oh, what *joy* for those
whose disobedience is *forgiven*,
 whose sin is put out of sight!
² Yes, what joy for those
  whose record the LORD has cleared of guilt,
  whose lives are lived in complete honesty!
³ When I refused to confess my sin,
  my body wasted away,
  and I groaned all day long.
⁴ Day and night your hand of discipline was heavy on me.
  My strength evaporated like water in the summer heat. *Interlude*

⁵ Finally, I confessed all my sins to you
  and stopped trying to hide my guilt.
 I said to myself, "I will confess my rebellion to the LORD."
  And you forgave me! All my guilt is gone. *Interlude*

⁶ Therefore, let all the godly pray to you while there is still time,
  that they may not drown in the floodwaters of judgment.
⁷ For you are my *hiding place;*
  you *protect me* from trouble.
   You surround me with
     songs of victory. *Interlude*

⁸ The LORD says, "I will guide you along the best pathway for your life.
  I will advise you and watch over you.
⁹ Do not be like a senseless horse or mule
  that needs a bit and bridle to keep it under control."

¹⁰ Many sorrows come to the wicked,
  but unfailing love surrounds those who trust the LORD.

¹¹ So *rejoice in the Lord* and be glad,
   all you who obey him! Shout for *joy,*
 all you whose *hearts are pure!*

33 ¹ Let the godly sing for joy to the LORD;
    it is fitting for the pure to praise him.
² Praise the LORD with melodies on the lyre;
  make music for him on the ten-stringed harp.
³ Sing a new song of praise to him;
  play skillfully on the harp, and sing with joy.

For *you* are my *Hiding* *Place,* YOU *PROTECT* me from TROUBLE
PSALM 32:7

⁴*For the word of the LORD holds true,*
and we can trust everything he does.
⁵ He loves whatever is just and good;
the unfailing love of the LORD fills the earth.

⁶ The LORD merely spoke,
and the heavens were created.
He breathed the word,
and all the stars were born.
⁷ He assigned the sea its boundaries
and locked the oceans in vast reservoirs.
⁸ Let the whole world fear the LORD,
and let everyone stand in awe of him.
⁹ For when he spoke, the world began!
It appeared at his command.

¹⁰ The LORD frustrates the plans of the nations
and thwarts all their schemes.

¹¹*But the Lord's plans stand firm forever;*
his intentions can never be shaken.

¹² What joy for the nation whose God is the LORD,
whose people he has chosen as his inheritance.

¹³ The LORD looks down from heaven
and sees the whole human race.
¹⁴ From his throne he observes
all who live on the earth.
¹⁵ He made their hearts,
so he understands everything they do.
¹⁶ The best-equipped army cannot save a king,
nor is great strength enough to save a warrior.
¹⁷ Don't count on your warhorse to give you victory—
for all its strength, it cannot save you.

¹⁸ But the LORD watches over those who fear him,
those who rely on his unfailing love.
¹⁹ He rescues them from death
and keeps them alive in times of famine.

²⁰ We put our hope in the LORD.
He is our help and our shield.

²¹*In him our hearts rejoice,*
for we trust in his holy name.

²² Let your unfailing love surround us, LORD,
for our hope is in you alone.

Taste and SEE that the Lord is GOOD

PSALM 34:8

34

A psalm of David, regarding the time he pretended to be insane in front of Abimelech, who sent him away.

¹ I will praise the LORD at all times.
    I will constantly speak his praises.
² I will boast only in the LORD;
    let all who are helpless take heart.
³ Come, let us tell of the LORD's greatness;
    let us exalt his name together.

⁴ *I prayed* to the LORD,
        and he answered me.
    He freed me from all my fears.
⁵ Those who look to him for help will be radiant with joy;
    no shadow of shame will darken their faces.
⁶ In my desperation I prayed, and the LORD listened;
    he saved me from all my troubles.
⁷ For the angel of the LORD is a guard;
    he surrounds and defends all who fear him.

⁸ Taste and see that *the Lord is good.*
    Oh, the joys of those who take refuge in him!
⁹ Fear the LORD, you his godly people,
    for those who fear him will have all they need.
¹⁰ Even strong young lions sometimes go hungry,
    but those who trust in the LORD will lack no good thing.

¹¹ Come, my children, and listen to me,
    and I will teach you to fear the LORD.
¹² Does anyone want to live a life
    that is long and prosperous?
¹³ Then keep your tongue from speaking evil
    and your lips from telling lies!
¹⁴ Turn away from evil and do good.
    Search for peace, and work to maintain it.

¹⁵ The eyes of the LORD watch over those who do right;
    his ears are open to their cries for help.
¹⁶ But the LORD turns his face against those who do evil;
    he will erase their memory from the earth.
¹⁷ The LORD hears his people when they call to him for help.
    He rescues them from all their troubles.
¹⁸ *The Lord* is close to the brokenhearted;
    he rescues those
    whose spirits are crushed.

¹⁹ The righteous person faces many troubles,
    but the LORD comes to the rescue each time.

34 This psalm is a Hebrew acrostic poem; each verse begins with a successive letter of the Hebrew alphabet.

²⁰ For the LORD protects the bones of the righteous;
  not one of them is broken!

²¹ Calamity will surely destroy the wicked,
  and those who hate the righteous will be punished.
²² But the LORD will redeem those who serve him.
  No one who takes refuge in him will be condemned.

35 *A psalm of David.*

¹ O LORD, oppose those who oppose me.
  Fight those who fight against me.
² Put on your armor, and take up your shield.
  Prepare for battle, and come to my aid.
³ Lift up your spear and javelin
  against those who pursue me.
 Let me hear you say,
  "I will give you victory!"
⁴ Bring shame and disgrace on those trying to kill me;
  turn them back and humiliate those who want to harm me.
⁵ Blow them away like chaff in the wind—
  a wind sent by the angel of the LORD.
⁶ Make their path dark and slippery,
  with the angel of the LORD pursuing them.
⁷ I did them no wrong, but they laid a trap for me.
  I did them no wrong, but they dug a pit to catch me.
⁸ So let sudden ruin come upon them!
  Let them be caught in the trap they set for me!
  Let them be destroyed in the pit they dug for me.

⁹Then I will *rejoice in the Lord.*
 I will be glad because he *rescues me.*

¹⁰ With every bone in my body I will praise him:
  "LORD, who can compare with you?
 Who else rescues the helpless from the strong?
  Who else protects the helpless and poor from those who rob them?"

¹¹ Malicious witnesses testify against me.
  They accuse me of crimes I know nothing about.
¹² They repay me evil for good.
  I am sick with despair.
¹³ Yet when they were ill, I grieved for them.
  I denied myself by fasting for them,
  but my prayers returned unanswered.
¹⁴ I was sad, as though they were my friends or family,
  as if I were grieving for my own mother.
¹⁵ But they are glad now that I am in trouble;
  they gleefully join together against me.
 I am attacked by people I don't even know;
  they slander me constantly.

¹⁶ They mock me and call me names;
   they snarl at me.

¹⁷ How long, O Lord, will you look on and do nothing?
   Rescue me from their fierce attacks.
   Protect my life from these lions!

¹⁸ Then I will *thank you* in front of

the great assembly. I will *praise you*

   before all the people.

¹⁹ Don't let my treacherous enemies rejoice over my defeat.
   Don't let those who hate me without cause gloat over my sorrow.
²⁰ They don't talk of peace;
   they plot against innocent people who mind their own business.
²¹ They shout, "Aha! Aha!
   With our own eyes we saw him do it!"

²² *O Lord,*

you know all about this. Do not stay silent.

Do not abandon me now, *O Lord.*

²³ Wake up! Rise to my defense!
   Take up my case, my God and my Lord.
²⁴ Declare me not guilty, O Lord my God, for you give justice.
   Don't let my enemies laugh about me in my troubles.
²⁵ Don't let them say, "Look, we got what we wanted!
   Now we will eat him alive!"

²⁶ May those who rejoice at my troubles
   be humiliated and disgraced.
   May those who triumph over me
   be covered with shame and dishonor.
²⁷ But give great joy to those who came to my defense.
   Let them continually say, "Great is the Lord,
   who delights in blessing his servant with peace!"
²⁸ Then I will proclaim your justice,
   and I will praise you all day long.

36 *For the choir director: A psalm of David, the servant of the Lord.*

¹ Sin whispers to the wicked, deep within their hearts.
   They have no fear of God at all.
² In their blind conceit,
   they cannot see how wicked they really are.
³ Everything they say is crooked and deceitful.
   They refuse to act wisely or do good.
⁴ They lie awake at night, hatching sinful plots.
   Their actions are never good.
   They make no attempt to turn from evil.

⁵ Your *unfailing love,*
O Lᴏʀᴅ, *is as vast as the heavens;*
your faithfulness reaches beyond the clouds.
⁶ Your righteousness is like the mighty mountains,
your justice like the ocean depths.
You care for people and animals alike, O Lᴏʀᴅ.
⁷ How precious is your unfailing love, O God!
All humanity finds shelter
in the shadow of your wings.
⁸ You feed them from the abundance of your own house,
letting them drink from your river of delights.
⁹ For you are the fountain of life,
the light by which we see.

¹⁰ Pour out your unfailing love on those who love you;
give justice to those with honest hearts.
¹¹ Don't let the proud trample me
or the wicked push me around.
¹² Look! Those who do evil have fallen!
They are thrown down, never to rise again.

37 * *A psalm of David.*

¹ Don't worry about the wicked
or envy those who do wrong.
² For like grass, they soon fade away.
Like spring flowers, they soon wither.

³ Trust in the Lᴏʀᴅ and do good.
Then you will live safely in the land and prosper.

⁴ Take *delight in the Lord,*
and he will give you your
heart's desires.

⁵ Commit everything you do to the Lᴏʀᴅ.
Trust him, and he will help you.
⁶ He will make your innocence radiate like the dawn,
and the justice of your cause will shine like the
noonday sun.

⁷ *Be still* in the presence of *the Lord,*
and wait patiently for him to act.

Don't worry about evil people who prosper
or fret about their wicked schemes.

37 This psalm is a Hebrew acrostic poem; each stanza begins with a successive letter of the Hebrew alphabet.

FOR YOU ARE THE Fountain OF Life, THE Light BY WHICH WE See
PSALM 36:9

⁸ Stop being angry!
    Turn from your rage!
  Do not lose your temper—
    it only leads to harm.
⁹ For the wicked will be destroyed,
    but those who trust in the LORD will possess the land.

¹⁰ Soon the wicked will disappear.
    Though you look for them, they will be gone.
¹¹ The lowly will possess the land
    and will live in peace and prosperity.

¹² The wicked plot against the godly;
    they snarl at them in defiance.
¹³ But the Lord just laughs,
    for he sees their day of judgment coming.

¹⁴ The wicked draw their swords
    and string their bows
  to kill the poor and the oppressed,
    to slaughter those who do right.
¹⁵ But their swords will stab their own hearts,
    and their bows will be broken.

¹⁶ It is better to be godly and have little
    than to be evil and rich.
¹⁷ For the strength of the wicked will be shattered,
    but the LORD takes care of the godly.

¹⁸ *Day by day the Lord takes care of the innocent,*
    and they will receive an inheritance
        that lasts forever.

¹⁹ They will not be disgraced in hard times;
    even in famine they will have more than enough.

²⁰ But the wicked will die.
    The LORD's enemies are like flowers in a field—
    they will disappear like smoke.

²¹ The wicked borrow and never repay,
    but the godly are generous givers.
²² Those the LORD blesses will possess the land,
    but those he curses will die.

²³ *The Lord directs the steps of the godly.*

  He delights in every detail of their lives.

²⁴ Though they stumble, they will never fall,
    for the LORD holds them by the hand.

25 Once I was young, and now I am old.
 Yet I have never seen the godly abandoned
 or their children begging for bread.
26 The godly always give generous loans to others,
 and their children are a blessing.

27 Turn from evil and do good,
 and you will live in the land forever.
28 For the LORD loves justice,
 and he will never abandon the godly.

 He will keep them safe forever,
 but the children of the wicked will die.
29 The godly will possess the land
 and will live there forever.

30 The godly offer good counsel;
 they teach right from wrong.
31 They have made God's law their own,
 so they will never slip from his path.

32 The wicked wait in ambush for the godly,
 looking for an excuse to kill them.
33 But the LORD will not let the wicked succeed
 or let the godly be condemned when they are put on trial.

34 Put your *hope in the Lord.*
 Travel steadily along his path.

 He will honor you by giving you the land.
 You will see the wicked destroyed.

35 I have seen wicked and ruthless people
 flourishing like a tree in its native soil.
36 But when I looked again, they were gone!
 Though I searched for them, I could not find them!

37 Look at those who are honest and good,
 for a wonderful future awaits those who love peace.
38 But the rebellious will be destroyed;
 they have no future.

39 *The LORD rescues the godly;* he is
 their *fortress* in times of trouble.

40 The LORD helps them,
 rescuing them from the wicked.
 He saves them,
 and they find shelter in him.

Put your hope in the Lord

Psalm 37:34

38 *A psalm of David, asking God to remember him.*

¹ O LORD, don't rebuke me in your anger
or discipline me in your rage!
² Your arrows have struck deep,
and your blows are crushing me.
³ Because of your anger, my whole body is sick;
my health is broken because of my sins.
⁴ My guilt overwhelms me—
it is a burden too heavy to bear.
⁵ My wounds fester and stink
because of my foolish sins.
⁶ I am bent over and racked with pain.
All day long I walk around filled with grief.
⁷ A raging fever burns within me,
and my health is broken.
⁸ I am exhausted and completely crushed.
My groans come from an anguished heart.

⁹ You know what I long for, Lord;
you hear my every sigh.
¹⁰ My heart beats wildly, my strength fails,
and I am going blind.
¹¹ My loved ones and friends stay away, fearing my disease.
Even my own family stands at a distance.
¹² Meanwhile, my enemies lay traps to kill me.
Those who wish me harm make plans to ruin me.
All day long they plan their treachery.

¹³ But I am deaf to all their threats.
I am silent before them as one who cannot speak.
¹⁴ I choose to hear nothing,
and I make no reply.
¹⁵ For I am waiting for you, O Lord.
You must answer for me, O Lord my God.
¹⁶ I prayed, "Don't let my enemies gloat over me
or rejoice at my downfall."

¹⁷ I am on the verge of collapse,
facing constant pain.
¹⁸ But I confess my sins;
I am deeply sorry for what I have done.
¹⁹ I have many aggressive enemies;
they hate me without reason.
²⁰ They repay me evil for good
and oppose me for pursuing good.

²¹ Do not abandon me, O Lord.
Do not stand at a distance, my God.
²² Come quickly to help me,
O Lord my savior.

39 *For Jeduthun, the choir director: A psalm of David.*

¹ I said to myself, "I will watch *what I do*
and not sin in what I say. I will hold
my tongue when the ungodly are around me."

² But as I stood there in silence—
not even speaking of good things—
the turmoil within me grew worse.
³ The more I thought about it,
the hotter I got,
igniting a fire of words:
⁴ "LORD, remind me how brief my time on earth will be.
Remind me that my days are numbered—
how fleeting my life is.
⁵ You have made my life no longer than the width of my hand.
My entire lifetime is just a moment to you;
at best, each of us is but a breath." *Interlude*

⁶ We are merely moving shadows,
and all our busy rushing ends in nothing.
We heap up wealth,
not knowing who will spend it.

⁷ And so, *Lord,* where do I put my *hope?*
My only hope is in you.

⁸ Rescue me from my rebellion.
Do not let fools mock me.
⁹ I am silent before you; I won't say a word,
for my punishment is from you.
¹⁰ But please stop striking me!
I am exhausted by the blows from your hand.
¹¹ When you discipline us for our sins,
you consume like a moth what is precious to us.
Each of us is but a breath. *Interlude*

¹² *Hear my prayer, O Lord!*
Listen to my cries for help! Don't ignore my tears.
For I am your guest—
a traveler passing through,
as my ancestors were before me.
¹³ Leave me alone so I can smile again
before I am gone and exist no more.

And so, Lord, where do I put my HOPE? My only hope {is} {in} You

Psalm 39:7

I take joy in doing YOUR WILL, my God

PSALM 40:8

40 *For the choir director: A psalm of David.*

¹ I waited patiently for the Lord to help me,
  and he turned to me and heard my cry.
² He lifted me out of the pit of despair,
  out of the mud and the mire.
He set my feet on solid ground
  and steadied me as I walked along.
³ He has given me a *new song* to sing,
  a hymn of *praise to our God.*

Many will see what he has done and be amazed.
  They will put their trust in the Lord.

⁴ *Oh, the joys* of those who *trust the Lord,*
  who have no confidence in the proud
  or in those who worship idols.
⁵ O Lord my God, you have performed many wonders for us.
  Your plans for us are too numerous to list.
  You have no equal.
If I tried to recite all your wonderful deeds,
  I would never come to the end of them.

⁶ You take no delight in sacrifices or offerings.
  Now that you have made me listen, I finally understand—
  you don't require burnt offerings or sin offerings.
⁷ Then I said, "Look, I have come.
  As is written about me in the Scriptures:

⁸ *I take joy* in doing *your will, my God,*
  for your instructions are
  written on my heart."

⁹ I have told all your people about your justice.
  I have not been afraid to speak out,
    as you, O Lord, well know.
¹⁰ I have not kept the good news of your justice hidden in
    my heart;
  I have talked about your faithfulness and saving power.
I have told everyone in the great assembly
  of your unfailing love and faithfulness.

¹¹ Lord, don't hold back your tender mercies from me.
  Let your unfailing love and faithfulness always
    protect me.

¹² For troubles surround me—
 too many to count!
My sins pile up so high
 I can't see my way out.
They outnumber the hairs on my head.
 I have lost all courage.

¹³ Please, LORD, rescue me!
 Come quickly, LORD, and help me.
¹⁴ May those who try to destroy me
 be humiliated and put to shame.
May those who take delight in my trouble
 be turned back in disgrace.
¹⁵ Let them be horrified by their shame,
 for they said, "Aha! We've got him now!"

¹⁶ *But may all who search for you be filled with joy & gladness in you. May those who love your salvation repeatedly shout, "The LORD is great!"*

¹⁷ As for me, since I am poor and needy,
 let the Lord keep me in his thoughts.
You are my helper and my savior.
 O my God, do not delay.

41 *For the choir director: A psalm of David.*

¹ Oh, the joys of those who are kind to the poor!
 The LORD rescues them when they are in trouble.

² *The Lord protects them and keeps them alive.*

He gives them prosperity in the land

and rescues them from their enemies.

³ The LORD nurses them when they are sick
 and restores them to health.

⁴ *"O LORD," I prayed, "have mercy on me.*

Heal me, for I have sinned against you."

⁵ But my enemies say nothing but evil about me.
 "How soon will he die and be forgotten?" they ask.
⁶ They visit me as if they were my friends,
 but all the while they gather gossip,
 and when they leave, they spread it everywhere.
⁷ All who hate me whisper about me,
 imagining the worst.
⁸ "He has some fatal disease," they say.
 "He will never get out of that bed!"

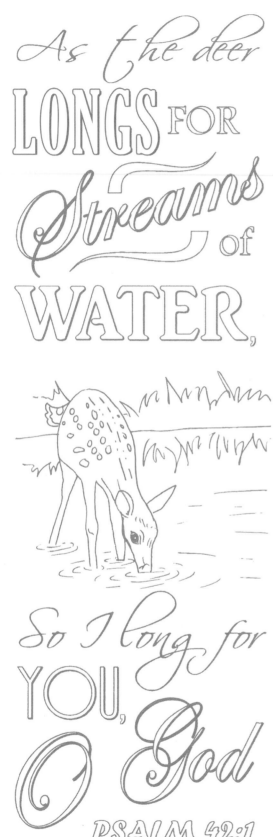

As the deer
LONGS FOR
Streams of
WATER,

So I long for
YOU,
O God

PSALM 42:1

⁹ Even my best friend, the one I trusted completely,
   the one who shared my food, has turned
      against me.

¹⁰ LORD, have mercy on me.
   Make me well again, so I can pay them back!
¹¹ I know you are pleased with me,
   for you have not let my enemies triumph over me.
¹² You have preserved my life because I am innocent;
   you have brought me into your presence forever.

¹³ Praise the LORD, the God of Israel,
   who lives from everlasting to everlasting.
Amen and amen!

BOOK TWO (Psalms 42–72)

42 *For the choir director: A psalm of the descendants of Korah.*

¹As the deer longs for *streams of water,*

   so I long for you, *O God.*

² I thirst for God, the living God.
   When can I go and stand before him?
³ Day and night I have only tears for food,
   while my enemies continually taunt me, saying,
   "Where is this God of yours?"

⁴ My heart is breaking
   as I remember how it used to be:
I walked among the crowds of worshipers,
   leading a great procession to the house of God,
singing for joy and giving thanks
   amid the sound of a great celebration!

⁵ Why am I discouraged?
   Why is my heart so sad?

I will put my *hope in God!*
   I will *praise him again—*
      my *Savior* and ⁶my *God!*

Now I am deeply discouraged,
   but I will remember you—
even from distant Mount Hermon, the source of the Jordan,
   from the land of Mount Mizar.
⁷ I hear the tumult of the raging seas
   as your waves and surging tides sweep over me.
⁸ But each day the LORD pours his unfailing love upon me,
   and through each night I sing his songs,
   praying to God who gives me life.

⁹ "O God my rock," I cry,
  "Why have you forgotten me?
Why must I wander around in grief,
  oppressed by my enemies?"
¹⁰ Their taunts break my bones.
  They scoff, "Where is this God of yours?"

¹¹ Why am I discouraged?
  Why is my heart so sad?
  I will put my hope in God!
  I will praise him again—
  my Savior and my God!

43 ¹ Declare me innocent, O God!
  Defend me against these ungodly people.
Rescue me from these unjust liars.
² For you are God, my only safe haven.
  Why have you tossed me aside?
Why must I wander around in grief,
  oppressed by my enemies?

³ Send out your *light* and your *truth;*
  let them guide me.
Let them lead me to your **holy mountain,**
  to the place where you live.
⁴ There I will go to the altar of God,
  to God—the source of all my joy.
I will praise you with my harp,
  O God, my God!

⁵ Why am I discouraged?
  Why is my heart so sad?
I will put my *hope in God!*
I will *praise* him again –
my Savior & my God!

44 *For the choir director: A psalm of the descendants of Korah.*

¹ O God, we have heard it with our own ears—
  our ancestors have told us
of all you did in their day,
  in days long ago:
² You drove out the pagan nations by your power
  and gave all the land to our ancestors.
You crushed their enemies
  and set our ancestors free.

³ They did not conquer the land with their swords;
    it was not their own strong arm that gave them victory.
  It was your right hand and strong arm
    and the blinding light from your face that helped them,
    for you loved them.

⁴ You are my King and my God.
    You command victories for Israel.
⁵ Only by your power can we push back our enemies;
    only in your name can we trample our foes.
⁶ I do not trust in my bow;
    I do not count on my sword to save me.

⁷ *You are the one who gives us*
            victory over our enemies;
        you disgrace those who hate us.
⁸ O God, we give glory to you all day long
    and constantly praise your name.   *Interlude*

⁹ But now you have tossed us aside in dishonor.
    You no longer lead our armies to battle.
¹⁰ You make us retreat from our enemies
    and allow those who hate us to plunder our land.
¹¹ You have butchered us like sheep
    and scattered us among the nations.
¹² You sold your precious people for a pittance,
    making nothing on the sale.
¹³ You let our neighbors mock us.
    We are an object of scorn and derision to those around us.
¹⁴ You have made us the butt of their jokes;
    they shake their heads at us in scorn.
¹⁵ We can't escape the constant humiliation;
    shame is written across our faces.
¹⁶ All we hear are the taunts of our mockers.
    All we see are our vengeful enemies.

¹⁷ All this has happened though we have not forgotten you.
    We have not violated your covenant.
¹⁸ Our hearts have not deserted you.
    We have not strayed from your path.
¹⁹ Yet you have crushed us in the jackal's desert home.
    You have covered us with darkness and death.
²⁰ If we had forgotten the name of our God
    or spread our hands in prayer to foreign gods,
²¹ God would surely have known it,
    for he knows the secrets of every heart.
²² But for your sake we are killed every day;
    we are being slaughtered like sheep.

²³ Wake up, O Lord! Why do you sleep?
    Get up! Do not reject us forever.
²⁴ Why do you look the other way?
    Why do you ignore our suffering and oppression?

²⁵ We collapse in the dust,
lying face down in the dirt.
²⁶ *Rise up! Help us!* Ransom us
because of your *unfailing love.*

45 *For the choir director: A love song to be sung to the tune "Lilies." A psalm of the descendants of Korah.*

¹ Beautiful words stir my heart.
I will recite a lovely poem about the king,
for my tongue is like the pen of a skillful poet.

² You are the most handsome of all.
Gracious words stream from your lips.
God himself has blessed you forever.
³ Put on your sword, O mighty warrior!
You are so glorious, so majestic!
⁴ In your majesty, ride out to victory,
defending truth, humility, and justice.
Go forth to perform awe-inspiring deeds!
⁵ Your arrows are sharp, piercing your enemies' hearts.
The nations fall beneath your feet.

⁶ *Your throne, O God, endures
forever and ever.
You rule with a scepter of justice.*

⁷ You love justice and hate evil.
Therefore God, your God, has anointed you,
pouring out the oil of joy on you more than on anyone else.
⁸ Myrrh, aloes, and cassia perfume your robes.
In ivory palaces the music of strings entertains you.
⁹ Kings' daughters are among your noble women.
At your right side stands the queen,
wearing jewelry of finest gold from Ophir!

¹⁰ Listen to me, O royal daughter; take to heart what I say.
Forget your people and your family far away.
¹¹ For your royal husband delights in your beauty;
honor him, for he is your lord.
¹² The princess of Tyre will shower you with gifts.
The wealthy will beg your favor.
¹³ The bride, a princess, looks glorious
in her golden gown.
¹⁴ In her beautiful robes, she is led to the king,
accompanied by her bridesmaids.
¹⁵ What a joyful and enthusiastic procession
as they enter the king's palace!

GOD HIMSELF HAS BLESSED YOU FOREVER

PSALM 45:2

¹⁶ Your sons will become kings like their father.
    You will make them rulers over many lands.
¹⁷ I will bring honor to your name in every generation.
    Therefore, the nations will praise you forever and ever.

46 *For the choir director: A song of the descendants of Korah, to be sung by soprano voices.*

¹ God is our *refuge & strength,*

always ready *to help* in times of trouble.

² So we will not fear when earthquakes come
    and the mountains crumble into the sea.
³ Let the oceans roar and foam.
    Let the mountains tremble as the waters surge!   *Interlude*

⁴ A river brings joy to the city of our God,
    the sacred home of the Most High.
⁵ God dwells in that city; it cannot be destroyed.
    From the very break of day, God will protect it.
⁶ The nations are in chaos,
    and their kingdoms crumble!
  God's voice thunders,
    and the earth melts!
⁷ The LORD of Heaven's Armies is here among us;
    the God of Israel is our fortress.   *Interlude*

⁸ Come, see the glorious works of the LORD:
    See how he brings destruction upon the world.
⁹ He causes wars to end throughout the earth.
    He breaks the bow and snaps the spear;
    he burns the shields with fire.

¹⁰ *"Be still,* and know that *I am God!*
    I will be *honored* by every nation.
    I will be honored *throughout the world."*

¹¹ The LORD of Heaven's Armies is here among us;
    the God of Israel is our fortress.   *Interlude*

47 *For the choir director: A psalm of the descendants of Korah.*

¹ Come, everyone! Clap your hands!
    Shout to God with joyful praise!
² For the LORD Most High is awesome.
    He is the great King of all the earth.
³ He subdues the nations before us,
    putting our enemies beneath our feet.
⁴ He chose the Promised Land as our inheritance,
    the proud possession of Jacob's descendants, whom he loves.   *Interlude*

⁵ God has ascended with a mighty shout.
   The Lord has ascended with trumpets blaring.
⁶ Sing praises to God, sing praises;
   sing praises to our King, sing praises!

⁷ For God is *the King* over all the earth.
   Praise him with a *psalm.*
⁸ *God reigns* above the nations,
            sitting on his *holy throne.*
⁹ The rulers of the world have gathered together
   with the people of the God of Abraham.
   For all the kings of the earth belong to God.
   He is highly honored everywhere.

48 *A song. A psalm of the descendants of Korah.*

¹ How great is *the Lord,* how deserving
of *praise,* in the city of our God,
   which sits on *his holy mountain!*

² It is high and magnificent;
   the whole earth rejoices to see it!
   Mount Zion, the holy mountain,
      is the city of the great King!
³ God himself is in Jerusalem's towers,
   revealing himself as its defender.

⁴ The kings of the earth joined forces
   and advanced against the city.
⁵ But when they saw it, they were stunned;
   they were terrified and ran away.
⁶ They were gripped with terror
   and writhed in pain like a woman in
      labor.
⁷ You destroyed them like the mighty ships of
      Tarshish
   shattered by a powerful east wind.

⁸ We had heard of the city's glory,
   but now we have seen it ourselves—
   the city of the Lord of Heaven's Armies.
   It is the city of our God;
      he will make it safe forever.   *Interlude*

⁹ O God, we meditate on your unfailing love
   as we worship in your Temple.

PSALM 48:1

He is our GOD forever and ever, and he will GUIDE us UNTIL we DIE

PSALM 48:14

10 As your name deserves, *O God, you will be praised* to the ends of the earth.
Your strong *right hand* is filled with *victory.*
11 Let the people on Mount Zion rejoice.
 Let all the towns of Judah be glad
 because of your justice.

12 Go, inspect the city of Jerusalem.
 Walk around and count the many towers.
13 Take note of the fortified walls,
 and tour all the citadels,
 that you may describe them
 to future generations.
14 For that is what God is like.
 He is our God forever and ever,
 and he will guide us until we die.

49 *For the choir director: A psalm of the descendants of Korah.*

1 *Listen to this,* all you people!
Pay attention, everyone in the world!

2 High and low,
 rich and poor—listen!
3 For my words are wise,
 and my thoughts are filled with insight.
4 I listen carefully to many proverbs
 and solve riddles with inspiration from a harp.

5 Why should I fear when trouble comes,
 when enemies surround me?
6 They trust in their wealth
 and boast of great riches.
7 Yet they cannot redeem themselves from death
 by paying a ransom to God.
8 Redemption does not come so easily,
 for no one can ever pay enough
9 to live forever
 and never see the grave.

10 *Those who are wise* must finally die,
 just like the foolish and senseless,
 leaving all *their wealth* behind.
11 The grave is their eternal home,
 where they will stay forever.
 They may name their estates after themselves,

¹² but their fame will not last.
   They will die, just like animals.
¹³ This is the fate of fools,
   though they are remembered as being wise.   *Interlude*

¹⁴ Like sheep, they are led to the grave,
   where death will be their shepherd.
 In the morning the godly will rule over them.
   Their bodies will rot in the grave,
   far from their grand estates.
¹⁵But as for me, *God will redeem my life.*

   He will snatch me *from the power* of the grave.   *Interlude*

¹⁶ So don't be dismayed when the wicked grow rich
   and their homes become ever more splendid.
¹⁷ For when they die, they take nothing with them.
   Their wealth will not follow them into the grave.
¹⁸ In this life they consider themselves fortunate
   and are applauded for their success.
¹⁹ But they will die like all before them
   and never again see the light of day.
²⁰ People who boast of their wealth don't
      understand;
   they will die, just like animals.

50 *A psalm of Asaph.*

¹ The Lord, the Mighty One, is God,
   and he has spoken;
 he has summoned all humanity
   from where the sun rises to where it sets.
² From Mount Zion, the perfection of beauty,
   God shines in glorious radiance.
³ Our God approaches,
   and he is not silent.
 Fire devours everything in his way,
   and a great storm rages around him.
⁴ He calls on the heavens above and earth below
   to witness the judgment of his people.
⁵ "Bring my faithful people to me—
   those who made a covenant with me by giving
      sacrifices."
⁶ Then let the heavens proclaim his justice,
   for God himself will be the judge.   *Interlude*

⁷ "O my people, listen as I speak.
   Here are my charges against you, O Israel:
   I am God, your God!
⁸ I have no complaint about your sacrifices
   or the burnt offerings you constantly offer.

Then CALL on me when You are in TROUBLE, AND I will Rescue YOU

PSALM 50:15

⁹ But I do not need the bulls from your barns
   or the goats from your pens.
¹⁰ For all the animals of the forest are mine,
   and I own the cattle on a thousand hills.
¹¹ I know every bird on the mountains,
   and all the animals of the field are mine.
¹² If I were hungry, I would not tell you,
   for all the world is mine and everything in it.
¹³ Do I eat the meat of bulls?
   Do I drink the blood of goats?
¹⁴ Make thankfulness your sacrifice to God,
   and keep the vows you made to the Most High.

¹⁵ Then call on me *when you are in trouble,*
   and I will *rescue you,*
   and you will give me *glory.* "

¹⁶ But God says to the wicked:
   "Why bother reciting my decrees
   and pretending to obey my covenant?
¹⁷ For you refuse my discipline
   and treat my words like trash.
¹⁸ When you see thieves, you approve of them,
   and you spend your time with adulterers.
¹⁹ Your mouth is filled with wickedness,
   and your tongue is full of lies.
²⁰ You sit around and slander your brother—
   your own mother's son.
²¹ While you did all this, I remained silent,
   and you thought I didn't care.
   But now I will rebuke you,
   listing all my charges against you.
²² Repent, all of you who forget me,
   or I will tear you apart,
   and no one will help you.
²³ *But giving thanks* is a sacrifice that truly
   honors me. If you keep to my path, I will
   reveal to you the *salvation* of God. "

51 *For the choir director: A psalm of David, regarding the time Nathan the prophet came to him after David had committed adultery with Bathsheba.*

¹ Have mercy on me, O God,
   because of your unfailing love.
   Because of your great compassion,
   blot out the stain of my sins.
² Wash me clean from my guilt.
   Purify me from my sin.

³ For I recognize my rebellion;
  it haunts me day and night.
⁴ Against you, and you alone, have I sinned;
  I have done what is evil in your sight.
  You will be proved right in what you say,
  and your judgment against me is just.
⁵ For I was born a sinner—
  yes, from the moment my mother conceived me.
⁶ But you desire honesty from the womb,
  teaching me wisdom even there.

⁷ *Purify me* from my sins,
    and I will be clean; *wash me,*
  and I will be *whiter than snow.*

⁸ Oh, give me back my joy again;
  you have broken me—
  now let me rejoice.
⁹ Don't keep looking at my sins.
  Remove the stain of my guilt.

¹⁰ *Create* in me a clean *heart, O God.*

  Renew a *loyal spirit* within me.

¹¹ Do not banish me from your presence,
  and don't take your Holy Spirit from me.

¹² Restore to me the joy of your salvation,
  and make me willing to obey you.
¹³ Then I will teach your ways to rebels,
  and they will return to you.
¹⁴ Forgive me for shedding blood, O God who saves;
  then I will joyfully sing of your forgiveness.
¹⁵ Unseal my lips, O Lord,
  that my mouth may praise you.

¹⁶ You do not desire a sacrifice, or I would offer one.
  You do not want a burnt offering.

¹⁷ *The sacrifice you desire is a broken spirit.*

  You will not reject a broken and repentant heart,
    O God.

¹⁸ Look with favor on Zion and help her;
  rebuild the walls of Jerusalem.
¹⁹ Then you will be pleased with sacrifices offered in the right spirit—
  with burnt offerings and whole burnt offerings.
  Then bulls will again be sacrificed on your altar.

Create in me a clean Heart, O God. RENEW A LOYAL SPIRIT within me.

Psalm 51:10

52

For the choir director: A psalm of David, regarding the time Doeg the Edomite said to Saul, "David has gone to see Ahimelech."

¹ Why do you boast about your crimes, great warrior?

Don't you realize *God's justice continues forever?*

² All day long you plot destruction.
    Your tongue cuts like a sharp razor;
    you're an expert at telling lies.
³ You love evil more than good
    and lies more than truth.   *Interlude*

⁴ You love to destroy others with your words,
    you liar!
⁵ But God will strike you down once and for all.
    He will pull you from your home
    and uproot you from the land of the living.   *Interlude*

⁶ The righteous will see it and be amazed.
    They will laugh and say,
⁷ "Look what happens to mighty warriors
    who do not trust in God.
  They trust their wealth instead
    and grow more and more bold in their wickedness."

⁸ But I am like an *olive tree*, thriving in the *house of God.* I will always *trust in God's unfailing love.*

⁹ I will praise you forever, O God,
    for what you have done.
  I will trust in your good name
    in the presence of your faithful people.

53

For the choir director: A meditation; a psalm of David.

¹ Only fools say in their hearts,
    "There is no God."
  They are corrupt, and their actions are evil;
    not one of them does good!

² *God* looks down from *heaven*
    on the entire *human race;*
  he looks to see if anyone is truly wise,
    if anyone seeks God.

PSALM 54:4

³ But no, all have turned away;
   all have become corrupt.
 No one does good,
   not a single one!

⁴ Will those who do evil never learn?
   They eat up my people like bread
   and wouldn't think of praying to God.
⁵ Terror will grip them,
   terror like they have never known before.
 God will scatter the bones of your enemies.
   You will put them to shame, for God has rejected them.

⁶ Who will come from Mount Zion to rescue Israel?
   When God restores his people,
   Jacob will shout with joy, and Israel will rejoice.

54 *For the choir director: A psalm of David, regarding the time the Ziphites came and said to Saul, "We know where David is hiding." To be accompanied by stringed instruments.*

¹ Come with great power, O God, and rescue me!
   Defend me with your might.
² Listen to my prayer, O God.
   Pay attention to my plea.
³ For strangers are attacking me;
   violent people are trying to kill me.
   They care nothing for God.   *Interlude*

⁴ *But God is my helper.*
   The Lord keeps me alive!

⁵ May the evil plans of my enemies be turned against them.
   Do as you promised and put an end to them.

⁶ I will sacrifice a voluntary offering to you;
   I will praise your name, O Lord,
   for it is good.
⁷ *For you have rescued me from my troubles*

   and helped me to triumph over my enemies.

55 *For the choir director: A psalm of David, to be accompanied by stringed instruments.*

¹ Listen to my prayer, O God.
   Do not ignore my cry for help!
² Please listen and answer me,
   for I am overwhelmed by my troubles.
³ My enemies shout at me,
   making loud and wicked threats.
 They bring trouble on me
   and angrily hunt me down.

4 My heart pounds in my chest.
　　The terror of death assaults me.
5 Fear and trembling overwhelm me,
　　and I can't stop shaking.
6 *Oh, that I had wings like a dove;*
　　then I would fly away and rest!

7 *I would fly far away*
　　to the quiet of the wilderness.　　　　　　*Interlude*

8 How quickly I would escape—
　　far from this wild storm of hatred.

9 Confuse them, Lord, and frustrate their plans,
　　for I see violence and conflict in the city.
10 Its walls are patrolled day and night against invaders,
　　but the real danger is wickedness within the city.
11 Everything is falling apart;
　　threats and cheating are rampant in the streets.

12 It is not an enemy who taunts me—
　　I could bear that.
　It is not my foes who so arrogantly insult me—
　　I could have hidden from them.
13 Instead, it is you—my equal,
　　my companion and close friend.
14 What good fellowship we once enjoyed
　　as we walked together to the house of God.

15 Let death stalk my enemies;
　　let the grave swallow them alive,
　　for evil makes its home within them.

16 But I will call on God,
　　and the LORD will rescue me.
17 *Morning, noon, and night*
　　I cry out in my distress,

　　and the LORD *hears my voice.*

18 He ransoms me and keeps me safe
　　from the battle waged against me,
　　though many still oppose me.
19 God, who has ruled forever,
　　will hear me and humble them.　　　　　　*Interlude*
　For my enemies refuse to change their ways;
　　they do not fear God.

20 As for my companion, he betrayed his friends;
　　he broke his promises.

Give your burdens to the Lord, and he will take care of you

PSALM 55:22

21 His words are as smooth as butter,
  but in his heart is war.
His words are as soothing as lotion,
  but underneath are daggers!

22 Give your burdens to *the Lord,* and he will *take care of you.* He will not permit *the godly* to slip and fall.

23 But you, O God, will send the wicked
  down to the pit of destruction.
Murderers and liars will die young,
  but I am trusting you to save me.

56 *For the choir director: A psalm of David, regarding the time the Philistines seized him in Gath. To be sung to the tune "Dove on Distant Oaks."*

1 O God, *have mercy* on me,
  for people are hounding me.
My foes attack me all day long.
2 I am constantly hounded by those who slander me,
  and many are boldly attacking me.
3 But when I am afraid,
  I will put my trust in you.
4 I praise God for what he has promised.
  I trust in God, so why should I be afraid?
  What can mere mortals do to me?

5 They are always twisting what I say;
  they spend their days plotting to harm me.
6 They come together to spy on me—
  watching my every step, eager to kill me.
7 Don't let them get away with their wickedness;
  in your anger, O God, bring them down.

8 You keep track of all my sorrows.
  You have collected all my tears in your bottle.
  You have recorded each one in your book.

9 My enemies will retreat when I call to you for help.
  This I know: God is on my side!

10 *I praise God* for what he has *promised;*
  yes, I *praise* the Lord
for what he has *promised.*

¹¹ I trust in God, so why should I be afraid?
　　What can mere mortals do to me?

¹² I will fulfill my vows to you, O God,
　　and will offer a sacrifice of thanks for your help.
¹³ For you have rescued me from death;
　　you have kept my feet from slipping.
So now I can walk *in your presence,*

O God, in your life-giving *light.*

57 *For the choir director: A psalm of David, regarding the time he fled from Saul and went into the cave. To be sung to the tune "Do Not Destroy!"*

¹ Have mercy on me, O God, have mercy!
　　I look to you for protection.
I will hide beneath the shadow of your
wings until the danger *passes by.*

² I cry out to God Most High,
　　to God who will fulfill his purpose for me.
³ He will send help from heaven to rescue me,
　　disgracing those who hound me.　　　　　　　　　　*Interlude*
　My God will send forth his unfailing love and faithfulness.

⁴ I am surrounded by fierce lions
　　who greedily devour human prey—
　whose teeth pierce like spears and arrows,
　　and whose tongues cut like swords.

⁵ Be exalted, O God, above the highest heavens!
　　May your glory shine over all the earth.

⁶ My enemies have set a trap for me.
　　I am weary from distress.
　They have dug a deep pit in my path,
　　but they themselves have fallen into it.　　　　　*Interlude*

⁷*My heart* is confident in you, *O God;*
　　　my heart is confident.
　　No wonder I can *sing your praises!*

⁸ Wake up, my heart!
　　Wake up, O lyre and harp!
　　I will wake the dawn with my song.
⁹ I will thank you, Lord, among all the people.
　　I will sing your praises among the nations.
¹⁰ For your unfailing love is as high as the heavens.
　　Your faithfulness reaches to the clouds.

¹¹Be exalted, *O God,* above the highest *heavens.*

May your *glory* shine over all the earth.

58 *For the choir director: A psalm of David, to be sung to the tune "Do Not Destroy!"*

¹ Justice—do you rulers know the meaning of the word?
　　Do you judge the people fairly?
² No! You plot injustice in your hearts.
　　You spread violence throughout the land.
³ These wicked people are born sinners;
　　even from birth they have lied and gone their own way.
⁴ They spit venom like deadly snakes;
　　they are like cobras that refuse to listen,
⁵ ignoring the tunes of the snake charmers,
　　no matter how skillfully they play.

⁶ Break off their fangs, O God!
　　Smash the jaws of these lions, O LORD!
⁷ May they disappear like water into thirsty ground.
　　Make their weapons useless in their hands.
⁸ May they be like snails that dissolve into slime,
　　like a stillborn child who will never see the sun.
⁹ God will sweep them away, both young and old,
　　faster than a pot heats over burning thorns.

¹⁰ The godly will rejoice when they see injustice avenged.
　　They will wash their feet in the blood of the wicked.
¹¹ Then at last everyone will say,

"There truly is a *reward* for those
　who *live for God;* surely there is a *God*
　　who judges justly here on earth."

59 *For the choir director: A psalm of David, regarding the time Saul sent soldiers to watch David's house in order to kill him. To be sung to the tune "Do Not Destroy!"*

¹ Rescue me from my enemies, O God.
　　Protect me from those who have come to destroy me.
² Rescue me from these criminals;
　　save me from these murderers.
³ They have set an ambush for me.
　　Fierce enemies are out there waiting, LORD,
　　though I have not sinned or offended them.
⁴ I have done nothing wrong,
　　yet they prepare to attack me.
　　Wake up! See what is happening and help me!

5 O LORD God of Heaven's Armies, the God of Israel,
   wake up and punish those hostile nations.
   Show no mercy to wicked traitors.

6 They come out at night,
   snarling like vicious dogs
   as they prowl the streets.
7 Listen to the filth that comes from their mouths;
   their words cut like swords.
   "After all, who can hear us?" they sneer.
8 But LORD, you laugh at them.
   You scoff at all the hostile nations.

9 *You are my strength; I wait for you to rescue me, for you, O God, are my fortress.*

10 In his unfailing love, my God will stand with me.
    He will let me look down in triumph on all my enemies.

11 Don't kill them, for my people soon forget such lessons;
    stagger them with your power, and bring them to their knees,
    O Lord our shield.
12 Because of the sinful things they say,
    because of the evil that is on their lips,
    let them be captured by their pride,
    their curses, and their lies.
13 Destroy them in your anger!
    Wipe them out completely!
    Then the whole world will know
    that God reigns in Israel.

14 My enemies come out at night,
    snarling like vicious dogs
    as they prowl the streets.
15 They scavenge for food
    but go to sleep unsatisfied.

16 *But as for me, I will sing about your power.
    Each morning I will sing with joy
    about your unfailing love.*

For you have been my refuge,
   a place of safety when I am in distress.
17 *O my Strength, to you I sing praises,
    for you, O God, are my refuge,
    the God who shows me unfailing love.*

Interlude

Interlude

Each MORNING I will SING with Joy about your UNFAILING Love

PSALM 59:16

60 *For the choir director: A psalm of David useful for teaching, regarding the time David fought Aram-naharaim and Aram-zobah, and Joab returned and killed 12,000 Edomites in the Valley of Salt. To be sung to the tune "Lily of the Testimony."*

¹ You have rejected us, O God, and broken our defenses.
    You have been angry with us; now restore us
        to your favor.
² You have shaken our land and split it open.
    Seal the cracks, for the land trembles.
³ You have been very hard on us,
    making us drink wine that sent us reeling.
⁴ But you have raised a banner for those who fear you—
    a rallying point in the face of attack.   *Interlude*

⁵ Now rescue your beloved people.
    Answer and save us by your power.

⁶ *God has promised* this by *his holiness:*
"I will divide up Shechem with joy.
    I will measure out the valley of Succoth.
⁷ Gilead is mine,
    and Manasseh, too.
  Ephraim, my helmet, will produce my warriors,
    and Judah, my scepter, will produce my kings.
⁸ But Moab, my washbasin, will become my servant,
    and I will wipe my feet on Edom
    and shout in triumph over Philistia."

⁹ Who will bring me into the fortified city?
    Who will bring me victory over Edom?
¹⁰ Have you rejected us, O God?
    Will you no longer march with our armies?
¹¹ Oh, please help us against our enemies,
    for all human help is useless.
¹² With God's help we will do mighty things,
    for he will trample down our foes.

61 *For the choir director: A psalm of David, to be accompanied by stringed instruments.*

¹ *O God,* listen to my cry!
    Hear my prayer!

² From the ends of the earth,
    I cry to you for help
    when my heart is overwhelmed.
  Lead me to the towering rock of safety,

³ for you are my safe refuge,
a fortress where my enemies cannot reach me.

⁴ Let me *live forever* in your sanctuary,

safe beneath the *shelter of your wings!*   *Interlude*

⁵ For you have heard my vows, O God.
You have given me an inheritance reserved for those who
fear your name.
⁶ Add many years to the life of the king!
May his years span the generations!
⁷ May he reign under God's protection forever.
May your unfailing love and faithfulness watch over him.
⁸ Then I will sing praises to your name forever
as I fulfill my vows each day.

62 *For Jeduthun, the choir director: A psalm of David.*

¹ I wait quietly before God,
for my victory comes from him.

² He alone is my *rock & my salvation,*

my fortress where I will never be shaken.

³ So many enemies against one man—
all of them trying to kill me.
To them I'm just a broken-down wall
or a tottering fence.
⁴ They plan to topple me from my high position.
They delight in telling lies about me.
They praise me to my face
but curse me in their hearts.   *Interlude*

⁵ Let all that I am *wait quietly* before God,

for my hope is in him.

⁶ He alone is my rock and my salvation,
my fortress where I will not be shaken.
⁷ My victory and honor come from God alone.
He is my refuge, a rock where no enemy can reach me.
⁸ O my people, trust in him at all times.
Pour out your heart to him,
for God is our refuge.   *Interlude*

⁹ Common people are as worthless as a puff of wind,
and the powerful are not what they appear to be.
If you weigh them on the scales,
together they are lighter than a breath of air.

Let all that I am wait, quietly before GOD, for my HOPE is in him. Psalm 62:5

I sing for joy in the shadow of your wings

PSALM 63:7

10 Don't make your living by extortion
   or put your hope in stealing.
And if your wealth increases,
   don't make it the center of your life.

11 God has spoken plainly,
   and I have heard it many times:
Power, O God, belongs to you;
12   unfailing love, O Lord, is yours.

Surely you *repay* all people

according to what they have *done.*

63 *A psalm of David, regarding a time when David was in the wilderness of Judah.*

1 O God, you are my God;
   I earnestly search for you.
My soul thirsts for you;
   my whole body longs for you
in this parched and weary land
   where there is no water.
2 I have seen you in your sanctuary
   and gazed upon your power and glory.

3 *Your unfailing love is better than life itself;* how I *praise you!*

4 I will praise you as long as I live,
   lifting up my hands to you in prayer.
5 You satisfy me more than the richest feast.
   I will praise you with songs of joy.

6 I lie awake thinking of you,
   meditating on you through the night.

7 Because you are *my helper,*

   I sing for *joy* in the shadow of your *wings.*

8 I cling to you;
   your strong right hand holds me securely.

9 But those plotting to destroy me will come to ruin.
   They will go down into the depths of the earth.
10 They will die by the sword
   and become the food of jackals.
11 But the king will rejoice in God.
   All who swear to tell the truth will praise him,
   while liars will be silenced.

64 *For the choir director: A psalm of David.*

¹ *O God,* listen to my complaint.
Protect my life from my enemies' threats.

² Hide me from the plots of this evil mob,
from this gang of wrongdoers.
³ They sharpen their tongues like swords
and aim their bitter words like arrows.
⁴ They shoot from ambush at the innocent,
attacking suddenly and fearlessly.
⁵ They encourage each other to do evil
and plan how to set their traps in secret.
"Who will ever notice?" they ask.
⁶ As they plot their crimes, they say,
"We have devised the perfect plan!"
Yes, the human heart and mind are cunning.

⁷ *But God himself* will shoot them
with his arrows, suddenly striking them down.

⁸ Their own tongues will ruin them,
and all who see them will shake their heads in scorn.
⁹ Then everyone will be afraid;
they will proclaim the mighty acts of God
and realize all the amazing things he does.
¹⁰ The godly will rejoice in the LORD
and find shelter in him.
And those who do what is right
will praise him.

65 *For the choir director: A song. A psalm of David.*

¹ What *mighty praise,* O God,
belongs to you in Zion.

We will fulfill our vows to you,
² for you answer our prayers.
All of us must come to you.
³ Though we are overwhelmed by our sins,
you forgive them all.
⁴ What joy for those you choose to bring near,
those who live in your holy courts.
What festivities await us
inside your holy Temple.

The
River of
God has
plenty
of water,
it provides a bountiful
harvest of grain,
for you have ordered it so.

Psalm 65:9

⁵ You faithfully answer our prayers with awesome deeds,
    O God our savior.

You are the *hope* of everyone *on earth,*

    even those who sail on *distant seas.*

⁶ You formed the mountains by your power
    and armed yourself with mighty strength.
⁷ You quieted the raging oceans
    with their pounding waves
    and silenced the shouting of the nations.
⁸ Those who live at the ends of the earth
    stand in awe of your wonders.
  From where the sun rises to where it sets,
    you inspire shouts of joy.

⁹ *You take care of the earth and water it, making it rich*

and fertile. The river *of God* has plenty of water;

    it provides a *bountiful harvest* of grain,

            for you have ordered it so.

¹⁰ You drench the plowed ground with rain,
    melting the clods and leveling the ridges.
  You soften the earth with showers
    and bless its abundant crops.
¹¹ You crown the year with a bountiful harvest;
    even the hard pathways overflow with
        abundance.
¹² The grasslands of the wilderness become a lush
        pasture,
    and the hillsides blossom with joy.

¹³ *The meadows are clothed with flocks of sheep,*

    and the valleys are carpeted with grain.

        They all shout and sing for joy!

66 *For the choir director: A song. A psalm.*

¹ Shout joyful praises to God, all the earth!
²   Sing about the glory of his name!
    Tell the world how glorious he is.
³ Say to God, "How awesome are your deeds!
    Your enemies cringe before your mighty power.
⁴ Everything on earth will worship you;
    they will sing your praises,
    shouting your name in glorious songs."   *Interlude*

⁵ Come and see what our God has done,
    what awesome miracles he performs for people!

May God be Merciful and Bless us.

May his face Smile with Favor on us

PSALM 67:1

⁶ He made a dry path through the Red Sea,
   and his people went across on foot.
   There we rejoiced in him.
⁷ For by his great power he rules forever.
   He watches every movement of the nations;
   let no rebel rise in defiance.   *Interlude*

⁸ Let the whole world bless our God
   and loudly sing his praises.
⁹ *Our lives* are in *his hands,*

and he keeps *our feet* from stumbling.

¹⁰ You have tested us, O God;
   you have purified us like silver.
¹¹ You captured us in your net
   and laid the burden of slavery on our backs.
¹² Then you put a leader over us.
   We went through fire and flood,
   but you brought us to a place of great abundance.

¹³ Now I come to your Temple with burnt offerings
   to fulfill the vows I made to you—
¹⁴ yes, the sacred vows that I made
   when I was in deep trouble.
¹⁵ That is why I am sacrificing burnt offerings to you—
   the best of my rams as a pleasing aroma,
   and a sacrifice of bulls and male goats.   *Interlude*

¹⁶ *Come and listen,* all you who fear *God,*

   and I will tell you *what he did* for me.
¹⁷ For I cried out to him for help,
   praising him as I spoke.
¹⁸ If I had not confessed the sin in my heart,
   the Lord would not have listened.
¹⁹ But God did listen!
   He paid attention to my prayer.
²⁰ Praise God, who did not ignore my prayer
   or withdraw his unfailing love from me.

67 *For the choir director: A song. A psalm, to be accompanied by stringed instruments.*

¹ May God be *merciful & bless us.*

   May his face *smile with favor on us.*   *Interlude*

² May your ways be known throughout the earth,
   your saving power among people everywhere.

³ May the nations praise you, O God.
   Yes, may all the nations praise you.
⁴Let the *whole world* *sing for joy,*

   because you govern the nations with justice
   and guide the people of the whole world.   *Interlude*

⁵ May the nations praise you, O God.
   Yes, may all the nations praise you.
⁶ Then the earth will yield its harvests,
   and God, our God, will richly bless us.
⁷ Yes, God will bless us,
   and people all over the world will fear him.

68 *For the choir director: A song. A psalm of David.*

¹ Rise up, O God, and scatter your enemies.
   Let those who hate God run for their lives.
² Blow them away like smoke.
   Melt them like wax in a fire.
   Let the wicked perish in the presence of God.
³*But let the godly rejoice.*

   Let them be glad in *God's presence.*

   Let them be filled with *joy.*

⁴ Sing praises to God and to his name!
   Sing loud praises to him who rides the clouds.
   His name is the LORD—
   rejoice in his presence!

⁵ Father to the fatherless, defender of widows—
   this is God, whose dwelling is holy.
⁶ God places the lonely in families;
   he sets the prisoners free and gives them joy.
   But he makes the rebellious live in a sun-scorched land.

⁷ O God, when you led your people out from Egypt,
   when you marched through the dry wasteland,   *Interlude*
⁸ the earth trembled, and the heavens poured down rain
   before you, the God of Sinai,
   before God, the God of Israel.
⁹*You sent abundant rain, O God,*
to refresh the weary land.

For each Day He carries us in His ARMS
PSALM 68:19

¹⁰*There your people finally settled,*
*and with a **bountiful harvest, O God,***
you provided for your needy people.

¹¹ The Lord gives the word,
and a great army brings the good news.
¹² Enemy kings and their armies flee,
while the women of Israel divide the plunder.
¹³ Even those who lived among the sheepfolds found treasures—
doves with wings of silver
and feathers of gold.
¹⁴ The Almighty scattered the enemy kings
like a blowing snowstorm on Mount Zalmon.

¹⁵ The mountains of Bashan are majestic,
with many peaks stretching high into the sky.
¹⁶ Why do you look with envy, O rugged mountains,
at Mount Zion, where God has chosen to live,
where the LORD himself will live forever?

¹⁷ Surrounded by unnumbered thousands of chariots,
the Lord came from Mount Sinai into his sanctuary.
¹⁸ When you ascended to the heights,
you led a crowd of captives.
You received gifts from the people,
even from those who rebelled against you.
Now the LORD God will live among us there.
¹⁹*Praise the Lord; praise God our savior!*

For each day he carries us in his arms. Interlude

²⁰ Our God is a God who saves!
The Sovereign LORD rescues us from death.

²¹ But God will smash the heads of his enemies,
crushing the skulls of those who love their guilty ways.
²² The Lord says, "I will bring my enemies down from Bashan;
I will bring them up from the depths of the sea.
²³ You, my people, will wash your feet in their blood,
and even your dogs will get their share!"

²⁴ Your procession has come into view, O God—
the procession of my God and King as he goes into the sanctuary.
²⁵ Singers are in front, musicians behind;
between them are young women playing tambourines.
²⁶ Praise God, all you people of Israel;
praise the LORD, the source of Israel's life.
²⁷ Look, the little tribe of Benjamin leads the way.
Then comes a great throng of rulers from Judah
and all the rulers of Zebulun and Naphtali.

²⁸ Summon your might, O God.
  Display your power, O God, as you have in the past.
²⁹ The kings of the earth are bringing tribute
  to your Temple in Jerusalem.
³⁰ Rebuke these enemy nations—
  these wild animals lurking in the reeds,
  this herd of bulls among the weaker calves.
  Make them bring bars of silver in humble tribute.
  Scatter the nations that delight in war.
³¹ Let Egypt come with gifts of precious metals;
  let Ethiopia bring tribute to God.

³² *Sing to God, you kingdoms* of the earth.
    Sing praises to the Lord.   *Interlude*

³³ Sing to the one who rides across the ancient heavens,
  his mighty voice thundering from the sky.
³⁴ Tell everyone about God's power.
  His majesty shines down on Israel;
  his strength is mighty in the heavens.
³⁵ God is awesome in his sanctuary.
  The God of Israel gives power and strength to his people.

Praise be to God!

69 *For the choir director: A psalm of David, to be sung to the tune "Lilies."*

¹ *Save me, O God,*
  for the floodwaters are up to my neck.
² Deeper and deeper I sink into the mire;
  I can't find a foothold.
  I am in deep water,
  and the floods overwhelm me.
³ I am exhausted from crying for help;
  my throat is parched.
  My eyes are swollen with weeping,
  waiting for my God to help me.
⁴ Those who hate me without cause
  outnumber the hairs on my head.
  Many enemies try to destroy me with lies,
  demanding that I give back what I didn't steal.

⁵ O God, you know how foolish I am;
  my sins cannot be hidden from you.
⁶ Don't let those who trust in you be ashamed because of me,
  O Sovereign Lord of Heaven's Armies.
  Don't let me cause them to be humiliated,
  O God of Israel.

Answer my PRAYERS. Take care of me, For your Mercy is so PLENTIFUL

PSALM 69:16

⁷ For I endure insults for your sake;
   humiliation is written all over my face.
⁸ Even my own brothers pretend they don't know me;
   they treat me like a stranger.

⁹ Passion for your house has consumed me,
   and the insults of those who insult you have fallen
      on me.
¹⁰ When I weep and fast,
   they scoff at me.
¹¹ When I dress in burlap to show sorrow,
   they make fun of me.
¹² I am the favorite topic of town gossip,
   and all the drunks sing about me.

¹³ But I keep *praying* to you, *Lord,* hoping this time
      you will *show me favor.* In your *unfailing love,*
   O *God,* answer my prayer with your sure *salvation.*
¹⁴ Rescue me from the mud;
   don't let me sink any deeper!
   Save me from those who hate me,
      and pull me from these deep waters.
¹⁵ Don't let the floods overwhelm me,
   or the deep waters swallow me,
   or the pit of death devour me.

¹⁶ Answer my *prayers, O Lord,* for your
            unfailing love *is wonderful.*
         Take care of me, for your mercy *is so plentiful.*
¹⁷ Don't hide from your servant;
   answer me quickly, for I am in deep trouble!
¹⁸ Come and redeem me;
   free me from my enemies.

¹⁹ You know of my shame, scorn, and disgrace.
   You see all that my enemies are doing.
²⁰ Their insults have broken my heart,
   and I am in despair.
   If only one person would show some pity;
      if only one would turn and comfort me.
²¹ But instead, they give me poison for food;
   they offer me sour wine for my thirst.

²² Let the bountiful table set before them become a snare
   and their prosperity become a trap.
²³ Let their eyes go blind so they cannot see,
   and make their bodies shake continually.
²⁴ Pour out your fury on them;
   consume them with your burning anger.
²⁵ Let their homes become desolate
   and their tents be deserted.

²⁶ To the one you have punished, they add insult to injury;
    they add to the pain of those you have hurt.
²⁷ Pile their sins up high,
    and don't let them go free.
²⁸ Erase their names from the Book of Life;
    don't let them be counted among the righteous.

²⁹ I am suffering and in pain.
    Rescue me, O God, by your saving power.

³⁰ Then I will praise God's name with singing,
    and I will honor him with thanksgiving.
³¹ For this will please the LORD more than sacrificing cattle,
    more than presenting a bull with its horns and hooves.

³² *The humble will see their God at work and be glad.*

Let all who seek God's help be encouraged.

³³ For the LORD hears the cries of the needy;
    he does not despise his imprisoned people.

³⁴ Praise him, O heaven and earth,
    the seas and all that move in them.
³⁵ For God will save Jerusalem
    and rebuild the towns of Judah.
His people will live there
    and settle in their own land.
³⁶ The descendants of those who obey him will inherit the land,
    and those who love him will live there in safety.

70 *For the choir director: A psalm of David, asking God to remember him.*

¹ Please, God, rescue me!
    Come quickly, LORD, and help me.
² May those who try to kill me
    be humiliated and put to shame.
May those who take delight in my trouble
    be turned back in disgrace.
³ Let them be horrified by their shame,
    for they said, "Aha! We've got him now!"

⁴ *But may all who search for you*

be filled with joy & gladness in you.

May those who love your salvation

repeatedly shout, "God is great!"

⁵ But as for me, I am poor and needy;
    please hurry to my aid, O God.
You are my helper and my savior;
    O LORD, do not delay.

71 ¹ O LORD, I have come to you for protection;
    don't let me be disgraced.
² Save me and rescue me,
    for you do what is right.
  Turn your ear to listen to me,
    and set me free.
³ Be my rock of safety
    where I can always hide.
  Give the order to save me,
    for you are my rock and my fortress.
⁴ My God, rescue me from the power of the wicked,
    from the clutches of cruel oppressors.

⁵ *O Lord, you alone are my hope.*

  I've trusted you, O Lord, from childhood.

⁶ Yes, you have been with me from birth;
    from my mother's womb you have cared for me.
  No wonder I am always praising you!

⁷ My life is an example to many,
    because you have been my strength and protection.

⁸ *That is why I can never stop praising you;*

  I declare your glory all day long.

⁹ And now, in my old age, don't set me aside.
    Don't abandon me when my strength is failing.
¹⁰ For my enemies are whispering against me.
    They are plotting together to kill me.
¹¹ They say, "God has abandoned him.
    Let's go and get him,
    for no one will help him now."

¹² O God, don't stay away.
    My God, please hurry to help me.
¹³ Bring disgrace and destruction on my accusers.
    Humiliate and shame those who want to harm me.
¹⁴ But I will keep on hoping for your help;
    I will praise you more and more.
¹⁵ I will tell everyone about your righteousness.
    All day long I will proclaim your saving power,
    though I am not skilled with words.
¹⁶ I will praise your mighty deeds, O Sovereign LORD.
    I will tell everyone that you alone are just.

¹⁷ O God, you have taught me from my earliest childhood,
    and I constantly tell others about the wonderful things you do.
¹⁸ Now that I am old and gray,
    do not abandon me, O God.
  Let me proclaim your power to this new generation,
    your mighty miracles to all who come after me.

¹⁹ Your righteousness, O God, reaches to the highest heavens.
You have done such wonderful things.
Who can compare with you, O God?
²⁰ You have allowed me to suffer much hardship,
but you will restore me to life again
and lift me up from the depths of the earth.
²¹ *You will restore me* to even *greater honor*

and *comfort* me once again.

²² Then I will praise you with music on the harp,
because you are faithful to your promises, O my God.
I will sing praises to you with a lyre,
O Holy One of Israel.
²³ I will shout for joy and sing your praises,
for you have ransomed me.
²⁴ *I will tell* about your
righteous deeds all day long,
for everyone who tried to hurt me
has been shamed and humiliated.

72 *A psalm of Solomon.*

¹ Give your **love of justice** to the king, *O God,*

and righteousness to the king's son.
² Help him judge your people in the right way;
let the poor always be treated fairly.
³ May the mountains yield prosperity for all,
and may the hills be fruitful.
⁴ Help him to defend the poor,
to rescue the children of the needy,
and to crush their oppressors.
⁵ May they fear you as long as the sun shines,
as long as the moon remains in the sky.
Yes, forever!

⁶ May the king's rule be refreshing like spring rain on freshly cut grass,
like the showers that water the earth.
⁷ May all the godly flourish during his reign.
May there be abundant prosperity until the moon is no more.
⁸ May he reign from sea to sea,
and from the Euphrates River to the ends of the earth.
⁹ Desert nomads will bow before him;
his enemies will fall before him in the dust.
¹⁰ The western kings of Tarshish and other distant lands
will bring him tribute.
The eastern kings of Sheba and Seba
will bring him gifts.

YOU will RESTORE me to even GreaTer HONOR
Psalm 71:21

PRAISE His glorious Name FOREVER!

PSALM 72:19

11 *All kings* will *bow* before him,
    and all nations will *serve him.*

12 He will rescue the poor when they cry to him;
    he will help the oppressed, who have no one to defend them.
13 He feels pity for the weak and the needy,
    and he will rescue them.
14 He will redeem them from oppression and violence,
    for their lives are precious to him.

15 Long live the king!
    May the gold of Sheba be given to him.
  May the people always pray for him
    and bless him all day long.
16 May there be abundant grain throughout the land,
    flourishing even on the hilltops.
  May the fruit trees flourish like the trees of Lebanon,
    and may the people thrive like grass in a field.
17 May the king's name endure forever;
    may it continue as long as the sun shines.
  May all nations be blessed through him
    and bring him praise.

18 Praise the LORD God, the God of Israel,
    who alone does such wonderful things.

19 *Praise his glorious name forever!*

  Let the whole earth be filled with *his glory.*
    Amen and amen!

20 (This ends the prayers of David son of Jesse.)

BOOK THREE (Psalms 73–89)

73 *A psalm of Asaph.*

1 Truly God is good to Israel,
    to those whose hearts are pure.
2 But as for me, I almost lost my footing.
    My feet were slipping, and I was almost gone.
3 For I envied the proud
    when I saw them prosper despite their wickedness.
4 They seem to live such painless lives;
    their bodies are so healthy and strong.
5 They don't have troubles like other people;
    they're not plagued with problems like everyone else.
6 They wear pride like a jeweled necklace
    and clothe themselves with cruelty.

7 These fat cats have everything
   their hearts could ever wish for!
8 They scoff and speak only evil;
   in their pride they seek to crush others.
9 They boast against the very heavens,
   and their words strut throughout the earth.
10 And so the people are dismayed and confused,
   drinking in all their words.
11 "What does God know?" they ask.
   "Does the Most High even know what's happening?"
12 Look at these wicked people—
   enjoying a life of ease while their riches multiply.

13 Did I keep my heart pure for nothing?
   Did I keep myself innocent for no reason?
14 I get nothing but trouble all day long;
   every morning brings me pain.

15 If I had really spoken this way to others,
   I would have been a traitor to your people.
16 So I tried to understand why the wicked prosper.
   But what a difficult task it is!

17 Then I went into *your sanctuary, O God,*

   and I finally understood *the destiny* of the wicked.

18 Truly, you put them on a slippery path
   and send them sliding over the cliff to destruction.
19 In an instant they are destroyed,
   completely swept away by terrors.
20 When you arise, O Lord,
   you will laugh at their silly ideas
   as a person laughs at dreams in the morning.

21 Then I realized that my heart was bitter,
   and I was all torn up inside.
22 I was so foolish and ignorant—
   I must have seemed like a senseless animal to you.

23 Yet I still *belong to you;*

   you hold my *right hand.*

24 You guide me with your counsel,
   leading me to a glorious destiny.
25 Whom have I in heaven but you?
   I desire you more than anything on earth.
26 My health may fail, and my spirit may grow weak,
   but God remains the strength of my heart;
   he is mine forever.

27 Those who desert him will perish,
   for you destroy those who abandon you.

28 But as for me, *how good it is* to be near God!
I have made the *Sovereign Lord* my shelter,
& I will tell everyone about the wonderful things you do.

74 *A psalm of Asaph.*

1 O God, why have you rejected us so long?
Why is your anger so intense against the sheep of your own pasture?
2 Remember that we are the people you chose long ago,
the tribe you redeemed as your own special possession!
And remember Jerusalem, your home here on earth.
3 Walk through the awful ruins of the city;
see how the enemy has destroyed your sanctuary.

4 There your enemies shouted their victorious battle cries;
there they set up their battle standards.
5 They swung their axes
like woodcutters in a forest.
6 With axes and picks,
they smashed the carved paneling.
7 They burned your sanctuary to the ground.
They defiled the place that bears your name.
8 Then they thought, "Let's destroy everything!"
So they burned down all the places where God was
worshiped.
9 *We no longer see your miraculous signs.*
All the prophets are gone, and no one can
tell us when it will end.
10 How long, O God, will you allow our enemies to insult you?
Will you let them dishonor your name forever?
11 Why do you hold back your strong right hand?
Unleash your powerful fist and destroy them.

12 *You, O God, are my king from ages past,*
bringing *salvation to the earth.*
13 You split the sea by your strength
and smashed the heads of the sea monsters.
14 You crushed the heads of Leviathan
and let the desert animals eat him.
15 You caused the springs and streams to gush forth,
and you dried up rivers that never run dry.

16 Both *day & night* belong to you;
you made the *starlight and the sun.*

Arise, O God, and DEFEND your cause

PSALM 74:22

¹⁷ You set the boundaries of the earth,
and you made both summer and winter.

¹⁸ See how these enemies insult you, LORD.
A foolish nation has dishonored your name.
¹⁹ Don't let these wild beasts destroy your turtledoves.
Don't forget your suffering people forever.

²⁰ Remember your covenant promises,
for the land is full of darkness and violence!
²¹ Don't let the downtrodden be humiliated again.
Instead, let the poor and needy praise your name.

²² *Arise, O God,* and defend your cause.

Remember how these fools insult you all day long.
²³ Don't overlook what your enemies have said
or their growing uproar.

75 *For the choir director: A psalm of Asaph. A song to be sung to the tune "Do Not Destroy!"*

¹ *We thank you, O God!*
We give thanks because you are near.

People everywhere tell of your wonderful deeds.

² God says, "At the time I have planned,
I will bring justice against the wicked.
³ When the earth quakes and its people live in turmoil,
I am the one who keeps its foundations firm.   *Interlude*

⁴ "I warned the proud, 'Stop your boasting!'
I told the wicked, 'Don't raise your fists!'
⁵ Don't raise your fists in defiance at the heavens
or speak with such arrogance.'"
⁶ For no one on earth—from east or west,
or even from the wilderness—
should raise a defiant fist.
⁷ It is God alone who judges;
he decides who will rise and who will fall.
⁸ For the LORD holds a cup in his hand
that is full of foaming wine mixed with spices.
He pours out the wine in judgment,
and all the wicked must drink it,
draining it to the dregs.

⁹ *But as for me,* I will always *proclaim*
what God has done; I will sing *praises*
to the God of Jacob.

¹⁰ For God says, "I will break the strength of the wicked,
    but I will increase the power of the godly."

76 *For the choir director: A psalm of Asaph. A song to be accompanied by stringed instruments.*

¹ God is honored in Judah;
    his name is great in Israel.
² Jerusalem is where he lives;
    Mount Zion is his home.
³ There he has broken the fiery arrows of the enemy,
    the shields and swords and weapons of war.   *Interlude*

⁴You are *glorious & more majestic*
than the *everlasting mountains*.

⁵ Our boldest enemies have been plundered.
    They lie before us in the sleep of death.
    No warrior could lift a hand against us.
⁶ At the blast of your breath, O God of Jacob,
    their horses and chariots lay still.

⁷No wonder *you are* greatly feared!
Who can stand before you when your anger explodes?

⁸ From heaven you sentenced your enemies;
    the earth trembled and stood silent before you.
⁹ You stand up to judge those who do evil, O God,
    and to rescue the oppressed of the earth.   *Interlude*
¹⁰ Human defiance only enhances your glory,
    for you use it as a weapon.

¹¹Make vows to *the Lord* your God, and keep them.
Let everyone bring *tribute* to the *Awesome One*.
¹² For he breaks the pride of princes,
    and the kings of the earth fear him.

77 *For Jeduthun, the choir director: A psalm of Asaph.*

¹ I cry out to God; yes, I shout.
    Oh, that God would listen to me!
² When I was in deep trouble,
    I searched for the Lord.
All night long I prayed,
with hands *lifted toward heaven*,
but my soul was not comforted.

O God, your ways are holy

PSALM 77:13

³ I think of God, and I moan,
overwhelmed with longing for his help. *Interlude*

⁴ You don't let me sleep.
I am too distressed even to pray!
⁵ I think of the good old days,
long since ended,
⁶ when my nights were filled with joyful songs.
I search my soul and ponder the difference now.
⁷ Has the Lord rejected me forever?
Will he never again be kind to me?
⁸ Is his unfailing love gone forever?
Have his promises permanently failed?
⁹ Has God forgotten to be gracious?
Has he slammed the door on his compassion? *Interlude*

¹⁰ And I said, "This is my fate;
the Most High has turned his hand against me."
¹¹ *But then I recall* all you have done, *O Lord;*
I remember your *wonderful deeds* of long ago.

¹² They are constantly in my thoughts.
I cannot stop thinking about your mighty works.

¹³ *O God,* your ways are *holy.*
Is there any god as mighty as you?
¹⁴ You are the God of great wonders!
You demonstrate your awesome power among the nations.
¹⁵ By your strong arm, you redeemed your people,
the descendants of Jacob and Joseph. *Interlude*

¹⁶ When the Red Sea saw you, O God,
its waters looked and trembled!
The sea quaked to its very depths.
¹⁷ The clouds poured down rain;
the thunder rumbled in the sky.
Your arrows of lightning flashed.
¹⁸ Your thunder roared from the whirlwind;
the lightning lit up the world!
The earth trembled and shook.
¹⁹ *Your road led through the sea, your pathway*
through the mighty waters ~ a pathway
no one knew was there!
²⁰ You led your people along that road like a flock of sheep,
with Moses and Aaron as their shepherds.

78 *A psalm of Asaph.*

¹ *O my people, listen* to my instructions.
  Open your ears to what I am saying,
² for I will speak to you in a parable.
 I will teach you hidden lessons from our past—
³ stories we have heard and known,
    stories our ancestors handed down to us.
⁴ We will not hide these truths from our children;
    we will tell the next generation
  about the glorious deeds of the LORD,
    about his power and his mighty wonders.
⁵ For he issued his laws to Jacob;
    he gave his instructions to Israel.
  He commanded our ancestors
    to teach them to their children,
⁶ so the next generation might know them—
    even the children not yet born—
    and they in turn will teach their own children.
⁷ So each generation should set its hope anew on God,
    not forgetting his glorious miracles
    and obeying his commands.
⁸ Then they will not be like their ancestors—
    stubborn, rebellious, and unfaithful,
    refusing to give their hearts to God.

⁹ The warriors of Ephraim, though armed with bows,
    turned their backs and fled on the day of battle.
¹⁰ They did not keep God's covenant
    and refused to live by his instructions.
¹¹ They forgot what he had done—
    the great wonders he had shown them,
¹² the miracles he did for their ancestors
    on the plain of Zoan in the land of Egypt.
¹³ For he divided the sea and led them through,
    making the water stand up like walls!
¹⁴ In the daytime he led them by a cloud,
    and all night by a pillar of fire.
¹⁵ He split open the rocks in the wilderness
    to give them water, as from a gushing spring.

¹⁶ *He made streams* pour from the rock,
  making the waters *flow down* like a *river!*

¹⁷ Yet they kept on sinning against him,
    rebelling against the Most High in the desert.
¹⁸ They stubbornly tested God in their hearts,
    demanding the foods they craved.
¹⁹ They even spoke against God himself, saying,
    "God can't give us food in the wilderness.

20 Yes, he can strike a rock so water gushes out,
   but he can't give his people bread and meat."
21 When the Lord heard them, he was furious.
   The fire of his wrath burned against Jacob.
   Yes, his anger rose against Israel,
22 for they did not believe God
   or trust him to care for them.
23 But he commanded the skies to open;
   he opened the doors of heaven.
24 He rained down manna for them to eat;
   he gave them bread from heaven.
25 They ate the food of angels!
   God gave them all they could hold.
26 He released the east wind in the heavens
   and guided the south wind by his mighty power.
27 He rained down meat as thick as dust—
   birds as plentiful as the sand on the seashore!
28 He caused the birds to fall within their camp
   and all around their tents.
29 The people ate their fill.
   He gave them what they craved.
30 But before they satisfied their craving,
   while the meat was yet in their mouths,
31 the anger of God rose against them,
   and he killed their strongest men.
   He struck down the finest of Israel's young men.

32 But in spite of this, the people kept sinning.
   Despite his wonders, they refused to trust him.
33 So he ended their lives in failure,
   their years in terror.
34 When God began killing them,
   they finally sought him.
   They repented and took God seriously.
35 Then they remembered that God was their rock,
   that God Most High was their redeemer.
36 But all they gave him was lip service;
   they lied to him with their tongues.
37 Their hearts were not loyal to him.
   They did not keep his covenant.
38 Yet he was merciful & forgave
   their sins and did not destroy them all.
Many times he held back his anger
   and did not unleash his fury!
39 For he remembered that they were merely mortal,
   gone like a breath of wind that never returns.

40 Oh, how often they rebelled against him in the wilderness
   and grieved his heart in that dry wasteland.

⁴¹ Again and again they tested God's patience
    and provoked the Holy One of Israel.
⁴² They did not remember his power
    and how he rescued them from their enemies.
⁴³ They did not remember his miraculous signs in Egypt,
    his wonders on the plain of Zoan.
⁴⁴ For he turned their rivers into blood,
    so no one could drink from the streams.
⁴⁵ He sent vast swarms of flies to consume them
    and hordes of frogs to ruin them.
⁴⁶ He gave their crops to caterpillars;
    their harvest was consumed by locusts.
⁴⁷ He destroyed their grapevines with hail
    and shattered their sycamore-figs with sleet.
⁴⁸ He abandoned their cattle to the hail,
    their livestock to bolts of lightning.
⁴⁹ He loosed on them his fierce anger—
    all his fury, rage, and hostility.
  He dispatched against them
    a band of destroying angels.
⁵⁰ He turned his anger against them;
    he did not spare the Egyptians' lives
    but ravaged them with the plague.
⁵¹ He killed the oldest son in each Egyptian family,
    the flower of youth throughout the land of Egypt.
⁵² But he led his own people like a flock of sheep,
    guiding them safely through the wilderness.
⁵³ He kept them safe so they were not afraid;
    but the sea covered their enemies.
⁵⁴ He brought them to the border of his holy land,
    to this land of hills he had won for them.
⁵⁵ He drove out the nations before them;
    he gave them their inheritance by lot.
  He settled the tribes of Israel into their homes.

⁵⁶ But they kept testing and rebelling against God Most High.
    They did not obey his laws.
⁵⁷ They turned back and were as faithless as their parents.
    They were as undependable as a crooked bow.
⁵⁸ They angered God by building shrines to other gods;
    they made him jealous with their idols.
⁵⁹ When God heard them, he was very angry,
    and he completely rejected Israel.
⁶⁰ Then he abandoned his dwelling at Shiloh,
    the Tabernacle where he had lived among the people.
⁶¹ He allowed the Ark of his might to be captured;
    he surrendered his glory into enemy hands.
⁶² He gave his people over to be butchered by the sword,
    because he was so angry with his own people—his special possession.
⁶³ Their young men were killed by fire;
    their young women died before singing their
      wedding songs.

He cared {for them with a} True Heart and led them with Skillful Hands

Psalm 78:72

⁶⁴ Their priests were slaughtered,
    and their widows could not mourn their deaths.

⁶⁵ Then the Lord rose up as though waking from sleep,
    like a warrior aroused from a drunken stupor.
⁶⁶ He routed his enemies
    and sent them to eternal shame.
⁶⁷ But he rejected Joseph's descendants;
    he did not choose the tribe of Ephraim.
⁶⁸ He chose instead the tribe of Judah,
    and Mount Zion, which he loved.
⁶⁹ There he built his sanctuary as high as the heavens,
    as solid and enduring as the earth.
⁷⁰ He chose his servant David,
    calling him from the sheep pens.
⁷¹ He took David from tending the ewes and lambs
    and made him the shepherd of Jacob's descendants—
    God's own people, Israel.
⁷² *He cared for them with a true heart*
    and led them with skillful hands.

79 *A psalm of Asaph.*

¹ O God, pagan nations have conquered your land,
    your special possession.
  They have defiled your holy Temple
    and made Jerusalem a heap of ruins.
² They have left the bodies of your servants
    as food for the birds of heaven.
  The flesh of your godly ones
    has become food for the wild animals.
³ Blood has flowed like water all around Jerusalem;
    no one is left to bury the dead.
⁴ We are mocked by our neighbors,
    an object of scorn and derision to those around us.

⁵ O Lord, how long will you be angry with us? Forever?
    How long will your jealousy burn like fire?
⁶ Pour out your wrath on the nations that refuse to acknowledge you—
    on kingdoms that do not call upon your name.
⁷ For they have devoured your people Israel,
    making the land a desolate wilderness.
⁸ Do not hold us guilty for the sins of our ancestors!
    Let your compassion quickly meet our needs,
    for we are on the brink of despair.

⁹ *Help us, O God of our salvation!*
    Help us for the *glory* of your name.

Save us and *forgive* our sins
for the honor of your name.

10 Why should pagan nations be allowed to scoff,
    asking, "Where is their God?"
  Show us your vengeance against the nations,
    for they have spilled the blood of your servants.
11 Listen to the moaning of the prisoners.
    Demonstrate your great power by saving those condemned to die.

12 O Lord, pay back our neighbors seven times
    for the scorn they have hurled at you.

13 Then we *your people,* the sheep of your pasture,
will *thank you forever and ever; praising*
  your greatness from generation to generation.

80 *For the choir director: A psalm of Asaph, to be sung to the tune
"Lilies of the Covenant."*

1 Please listen, O Shepherd of Israel,
    you who lead Joseph's descendants like a flock.
  O God, enthroned above the cherubim,
    display your radiant glory
2   to Ephraim, Benjamin, and Manasseh.

Show us your *mighty power.*

Come to *rescue us!*

3 Turn us again to yourself, O God.
    Make your face shine down upon us.
    Only then will we be saved.
4 O LORD God of Heaven's Armies,
    how long will you be angry with our prayers?
5 You have fed us with sorrow
    and made us drink tears by the bucketful.
6 You have made us the scorn of neighboring nations.
    Our enemies treat us as a joke.

7 *Turn us again to yourself, O God of
Heaven's Armies.* Make your face
  shine down upon us. Only then will we be *saved.*
8 You brought us from Egypt like a grapevine;
    you drove away the pagan nations and transplanted us into your land.
9 You cleared the ground for us,
    and we took root and filled the land.

O LORD, make your face shine down upon us

Psalm 80:19

¹⁰ Our shade covered the mountains;
   our branches covered the mighty cedars.
¹¹ We spread our branches west to the Mediterranean Sea;
   our shoots spread east to the Euphrates River.
¹² But now, why have you broken down our walls
   so that all who pass by may steal our fruit?
¹³ The wild boar from the forest devours it,
   and the wild animals feed on it.

¹⁴ Come back, we beg you, O God of Heaven's Armies.
   Look down from heaven and see our plight.
   Take care of this grapevine
¹⁵   that you yourself have planted,
   this son you have raised for yourself.
¹⁶ For we are chopped up and burned by our enemies.
   May they perish at the sight of your frown.
¹⁷ Strengthen the man you love,
   the son of your choice.
¹⁸ Then we will never abandon you again.
   Revive us so we can call on your name once more.

¹⁹ Turn us again to yourself, O LORD God of Heaven's Armies.

Make *your face shine down* upon us. Only then will we be *saved.*

81 *For the choir director: A psalm of Asaph, to be accompanied by a stringed instrument.*

¹ *Sing praises to God, our strength.*

   Sing to the God of Jacob.
² Sing! Beat the tambourine.
   Play the sweet lyre and the harp.
³ Blow the ram's horn at new moon,
   and again at full moon to call a festival!
⁴ For this is required by the decrees of Israel;
   it is a regulation of the God of Jacob.
⁵ He made it a law for Israel
   when he attacked Egypt to set us free.

   I heard an unknown voice say,
⁶ "Now I will take the load from your shoulders;
   I will free your hands from their heavy tasks.
⁷ You cried to me in trouble, and I saved you;
   I answered out of the thundercloud
   and tested your faith when there was no water at Meribah.   *Interlude*

⁸ "Listen to me, O my people, while I give you stern warnings.
   O Israel, if you would only listen to me!

⁹You must never have a foreign god;
you must not *bow down* before a false god.
¹⁰ For it was I, the LORD your God,
who rescued you from the land of Egypt.
Open your mouth wide, and I will fill it with good things.

¹¹ "But no, my people wouldn't listen.
Israel did not want me around.
¹² So I let them follow their own stubborn desires,
living according to their own ideas.
¹³ Oh, that my people would listen to me!
Oh, that Israel would follow me, walking in my paths!
¹⁴ How quickly I would then subdue their enemies!
How soon my hands would be upon their foes!
¹⁵ Those who hate the LORD would cringe before him;
they would be doomed forever.
¹⁶ *But I would feed you* with the *finest wheat.* I would
satisfy you with wild honey from *the rock.*"

82 *A psalm of Asaph.*

¹ God presides over heaven's court;
he pronounces judgment on the heavenly beings:
² "How long will you hand down unjust decisions
by favoring the wicked?   *Interlude*

³ "Give justice to the poor and the orphan;
uphold the rights of the oppressed and the destitute.
⁴*Rescue* the poor and helpless;
deliver them from the grasp of evil people.
⁵ But these oppressors know nothing;
they are so ignorant!
They wander about in darkness,
while the whole world is shaken to the core.
⁶ I say, 'You are gods;
you are all children of the Most High.
⁷ But you will die like mere mortals
and fall like every other ruler.'"

⁸*Rise up, O God,* and judge the earth,
for all the nations *belong to you.*

83 *A song. A psalm of Asaph.*

1 *O God,* do not be *silent!*

Do not be deaf.
Do not be quiet, O God.
2 Don't you hear the uproar of your enemies?
Don't you see that your arrogant enemies are
rising up?
3 They devise crafty schemes against your people;
they conspire against your precious ones.
4 "Come," they say, "let us wipe out Israel as a nation.
We will destroy the very memory of its existence."
5 Yes, this was their unanimous decision.
They signed a treaty as allies against you—
6 these Edomites and Ishmaelites;
Moabites and Hagrites;
7 Gebalites, Ammonites, and Amalekites;
and people from Philistia and Tyre.
8 Assyria has joined them, too,
and is allied with the descendants of Lot.   *Interlude*

9 Do to them as you did to the Midianites
and as you did to Sisera and Jabin at the Kishon River.
10 They were destroyed at Endor,
and their decaying corpses fertilized the soil.
11 Let their mighty nobles die as Oreb and Zeeb did.
Let all their princes die like Zebah and Zalmunna,
12 for they said, "Let us seize for our own use
these pasturelands of God!"

13 *O my God,* scatter them like tumbleweed,
like chaff *before the wind!*

14 As a fire burns a forest
and as a flame sets mountains ablaze,
15 chase them with your fierce storm;
terrify them with your tempest.
16 Utterly disgrace them
until they submit to your name, O LORD.
17 Let them be ashamed and terrified forever.
Let them die in disgrace.

18 Then they will *learn* that you alone are called
the Lord, that you alone are the
Most High, supreme over all the earth.

84
For the choir director: A psalm of the descendants of Korah, to be accompanied by a stringed instrument.

¹ How *lovely* is your dwelling place,
O Lord of Heaven's Armies.

² I long, yes, I faint with longing
   to enter the courts of the Lord.
 With my whole being, body and soul,
   I will shout joyfully to the living God.
³ Even the sparrow finds a home,
   and the swallow builds her nest and raises her young
 at a place near your altar,
   O Lord of Heaven's Armies, my King and my God!

⁴ What *joy* for those who can live in your house,
 always singing *your praises.*   *Interlude*

⁵ What joy for those whose strength comes from the Lord,
   who have set their minds on a pilgrimage to Jerusalem.
⁶ When they walk through the Valley of Weeping,
   it will become a place of refreshing springs.
   The autumn rains will clothe it with blessings.
⁷ They will continue to grow stronger,
   and each of them will appear before God in Jerusalem.

⁸ O Lord God of Heaven's Armies, hear my prayer.
   Listen, O God of Jacob.   *Interlude*

⁹ O God, look with favor upon the king, our shield!
   Show favor to the one you have anointed.

¹⁰ A single day in your courts
   is better than a thousand anywhere else!
 I would rather be a gatekeeper in the house of my God
   than live the good life in the homes of the wicked.

¹¹ For the *Lord God* is our sun and our shield.

 He gives us *grace & glory. The Lord will*
 withhold no good thing from those who do what is *right.*

¹² O Lord of Heaven's Armies,
   what joy for those who trust in you.

85
For the choir director: A psalm of the descendants of Korah.

¹ Lord, you poured out blessings on your land!
   You restored the fortunes of Israel.

For the Lord GOD is our sun and our shield

Psalm 84:11

A single day in your courts is better than a thousand anywhere else!

Psalm 84:10

² You forgave the guilt of your people—
    yes, you covered all their sins.
³ You held back your fury.
    You kept back your blazing anger.

                  Interlude

⁴ Now restore us again, O God of our salvation.
    Put aside your anger against us once more.
⁵ Will you be angry with us always?
    Will you prolong your wrath to all generations?
⁶ Won't you revive us again,
    so your people can rejoice in you?

⁷ *Show us your unfailing love, O Lord,*
    & grant us your salvation.

⁸ I listen carefully to what God the Lord is saying,
    for he speaks peace to his faithful people.
    But let them not return to their foolish ways.
⁹ Surely his salvation is near to those who fear him,
    so our land will be filled with his glory.

¹⁰ Unfailing love and truth have met together.
    Righteousness and peace have kissed!
¹¹ Truth springs up from the earth,
    and righteousness smiles down from heaven.

¹² *Yes, the Lord pours down his blessings.*
    Our land will yield its bountiful harvest.
¹³ Righteousness goes as a herald before him,
    preparing the way for his steps.

86 *A prayer of David.*

¹ Bend down, O Lord, and hear my prayer;
    answer me, for I need your help.
² Protect me, for I am devoted to you.
    Save me, for I serve you and trust you.
    You are my God.
³ Be merciful to me, O Lord,
    for I am calling on you constantly.

⁴ *Give me happiness, O Lord,*
    for I give myself to you.

⁵ O Lord, you are so good, so ready to forgive,
    so full of unfailing love for all who ask for your help.
⁶ Listen closely to my prayer, O Lord;
    hear my urgent cry.
⁷ I will call to you whenever I'm in trouble,
    and you will answer me.

Grant me
Purity
of
Heart,
so that
I MAY
Honor
YOU

Psalm 86:11

⁸ No pagan god is like you, O Lord.
　None can do what you do!
⁹ All the nations you made
　will come and bow before you, Lord;
　they will praise your holy name.
¹⁰ For you are great and perform wonderful deeds.
　You alone are God.

¹¹ Teach me your ways, *O Lord,*
　　　that I may live according to your *truth!*
Grant me *purity* of *heart,*
　　　so that I may *honor you.*
¹² With all my heart I will praise you, O Lord my God.
　I will give glory to your name forever,
¹³ for your love for me is very great.
　You have rescued me from the depths of death.

¹⁴ O God, insolent people rise up against me;
　a violent gang is trying to kill me.
　You mean nothing to them.
¹⁵ *But you,* O Lord, are a God of
　compassion & mercy, slow to get angry
　　and filled with *unfailing love* and faithfulness.

¹⁶ Look down and have mercy on me.
　Give your strength to your servant;
　save me, the son of your servant.
¹⁷ Send me a sign of your favor.
　Then those who hate me will be put to shame,
　for you, O Lord, help and comfort me.

87 *A song. A psalm of the descendants of Korah.*

¹ On the *holy* mountain
　　stands the city founded by *the Lord.*
² He loves the city of Jerusalem
　more than any other city in Israel.
³ O city of God,
　what glorious things are said of you!　　　　　　　*Interlude*

⁴ I will count Egypt and Babylon among those who know me—
　also Philistia and Tyre, and even distant Ethiopia.
　They have all become citizens of Jerusalem!
⁵ Regarding Jerusalem it will be said,
　"Everyone enjoys the rights of citizenship there."
　And the Most High will personally bless this city.

⁶ When the Lᴏʀᴅ registers the nations, he will say,
  "They have all become citizens of Jerusalem."   *Interlude*

⁷ The people will play flutes and sing,
  "The source of my life springs from Jerusalem!"

88 *For the choir director: A psalm of the descendants of Korah. A song to be sung to the tune "The Suffering of Affliction." A psalm of Heman the Ezrahite.*

¹ *O Lord,* God of my *salvation,*

  I cry out to you by *day.* *I come to you at* *night.*

² Now hear my prayer;
  listen to my cry.
³ For my life is full of troubles,
  and death draws near.
⁴ I am as good as dead,
  like a strong man with no strength left.
⁵ They have left me among the dead,
  and I lie like a corpse in a grave.
 I am forgotten,
  cut off from your care.
⁶ You have thrown me into the lowest pit,
  into the darkest depths.
⁷ Your anger weighs me down;
  with wave after wave you have engulfed me.   *Interlude*

⁸ You have driven my friends away
  by making me repulsive to them.
 I am in a trap with no way of escape.
⁹   My eyes are blinded by my tears.
 Each day I beg for your help, O Lᴏʀᴅ;

  I lift my hands

    to you for *mercy.*

¹⁰ Are your wonderful deeds of any use to the dead?
  Do the dead rise up and praise you?   *Interlude*

¹¹ Can those in the grave declare your unfailing love?
  Can they proclaim your faithfulness in the place of destruction?
¹² Can the darkness speak of your wonderful deeds?
  Can anyone in the land of forgetfulness talk about your righteousness?
¹³ O Lᴏʀᴅ, I cry out to you.
  I will keep on pleading day by day.
¹⁴ O Lᴏʀᴅ, why do you reject me?
  Why do you turn your face from me?

¹⁵ I have been sick and close to death since my youth.
  I stand helpless and desperate before your terrors.
¹⁶ Your fierce anger has overwhelmed me.
  Your terrors have paralyzed me.

17 They swirl around me like floodwaters all day long.
  They have engulfed me completely.
18 You have taken away my companions and loved ones.
  Darkness is my closest friend.

89 *A psalm of Ethan the Ezrahite.*

1 I will sing of the *Lord's* unfailing love forever!
Young and old will hear of your *faithfulness.*
  2 Your unfailing love will last *forever.*
    Your *faithfulness* is as enduring as the **heavens.**

3 The LORD said, "I have made a covenant with David, my chosen servant.
  I have sworn this oath to him:
4 'I will establish your descendants as kings forever;
  they will sit on your throne from now until eternity.'"

Interlude

5 All heaven will praise your great wonders, LORD;
  myriads of angels will praise you for your faithfulness.
6 For who in all of heaven can compare with the LORD?
  What mightiest angel is anything like the LORD?
7 The highest angelic powers stand in awe of God.
  He is far more awesome than all who surround his throne.
8 O LORD God of Heaven's Armies!
  Where is there anyone as mighty as you, O LORD?
  You are entirely faithful.

9 You rule the oceans.
  You subdue their storm-tossed waves.
10 You crushed the great sea monster.
  You scattered your enemies with your mighty arm.
11 The heavens are yours, and the earth is yours;
everything in the world is yours – you *created* it all.
12 You created north and south.
  Mount Tabor and Mount Hermon praise your name.
13 Powerful is your arm!
  Strong is your hand!
  Your right hand is lifted high in glorious strength.
14 Righteousness and justice are the foundation of your throne.
  Unfailing love and truth walk before you as attendants.
15 Happy are those who hear the joyful call to worship,
  for they will walk in the light of your presence, LORD.
16 They rejoice all day long in your wonderful reputation.
  They exult in your righteousness.

¹⁷ You are their glorious strength.
It pleases you to make us strong.
¹⁸ *Yes, our protection* comes from *the Lord,*

and he, *the Holy One* of Israel, has given us our *king.*

¹⁹ Long ago you spoke in a vision to your faithful people.
You said, "I have raised up a warrior.
I have selected him from the common people to be king.
²⁰ I have found my servant David.
I have anointed him with my holy oil.
²¹ I will steady him with my hand;
with my powerful arm I will make him strong.
²² His enemies will not defeat him,
nor will the wicked overpower him.
²³ I will beat down his adversaries before him
and destroy those who hate him.
²⁴ My faithfulness and unfailing love will be with him,
and by my authority he will grow in power.
²⁵ I will extend his rule over the sea,
his dominion over the rivers.
²⁶ *And he will call out to me,* '*You are my Father,*

my God, and the Rock of my *salvation.*'

²⁷ I will make him my firstborn son,
the mightiest king on earth.
²⁸ I will love him and be kind to him forever;
my covenant with him will never end.
²⁹ I will preserve an heir for him;
his throne will be as endless as the days of heaven.
³⁰ But if his descendants forsake my instructions
and fail to obey my regulations,
³¹ if they do not obey my decrees
and fail to keep my commands,
³² then I will punish their sin with the rod,
and their disobedience with beating.

³³ *But I will never stop loving him*

nor fail to keep my promise to him.

³⁴ No, I will not break my covenant;
I will not take back a single word I said.
³⁵ I have sworn an oath to David,
and in my holiness I cannot lie:
³⁶ His dynasty will go on forever;
his kingdom will endure as the sun.
³⁷ It will be as eternal as the moon,
my faithful witness in the sky!"   *Interlude*

You are my Father, my God, and the ROCK of my salvation

PSALM 89:26

³⁸ But now you have rejected him and cast him off.
　　You are angry with your anointed king.
³⁹ You have renounced your covenant with him;
　　you have thrown his crown in the dust.
⁴⁰ You have broken down the walls protecting him
　　and ruined every fort defending him.
⁴¹ Everyone who comes along has robbed him,
　　and he has become a joke to his neighbors.
⁴² You have strengthened his enemies
　　and made them all rejoice.
⁴³ You have made his sword useless
　　and refused to help him in battle.
⁴⁴ You have ended his splendor
　　and overturned his throne.
⁴⁵ You have made him old before his time
　　and publicly disgraced him.　　　　　　　　　　*Interlude*

⁴⁶ O Lord, how long will this go on?
　　Will you hide yourself forever?
　　How long will your anger burn like fire?
⁴⁷ Remember how short my life is,
　　how empty and futile this human existence!
⁴⁸ No one can live forever; all will die.
　　No one can escape the power of the grave.　　*Interlude*

⁴⁹ Lord, where is your unfailing love?
　　You promised it to David with a faithful pledge.
⁵⁰ Consider, Lord, how your servants are disgraced!
　　I carry in my heart the insults of so many
　　　people.
⁵¹ Your enemies have mocked me, O Lord;
　　they mock your anointed king wherever he goes.

⁵² *Praise the Lord forever!*

Amen and amen!

Book Four (Psalms 90–106)

90 *A prayer of Moses, the man of God.*

¹ Lord, through all the generations
　　you have been our home!
² Before the mountains were born,
　　before you gave birth to the earth and the world,
　　from beginning to end, you are God.

³ You turn people back to dust, saying,
　　"Return to dust, you mortals!"
⁴ For you, a thousand years are as a passing day,
　　as brief as a few night hours.

⁵ You sweep people away like dreams that disappear.
  They are like grass that springs up in the morning.
⁶ In the morning it blooms and flourishes,
  but by evening it is dry and withered.
⁷ We wither beneath your anger;
  we are overwhelmed by your fury.
⁸ You spread out our sins before you—
  our secret sins—and you see them all.
⁹ We live our lives beneath your wrath,
  ending our years with a groan.

¹⁰ Seventy years are given to us!
  Some even live to eighty.
  But even the best years are filled with pain and trouble;
  soon they disappear, and we fly away.
¹¹ Who can comprehend the power of your anger?
  Your wrath is as awesome as the fear you deserve.
¹² *Teach us* to realize the brevity of life,

  so that we may *grow in wisdom.*

¹³ O Lord, come back to us!
  How long will you delay?
  Take pity on your servants!
¹⁴ Satisfy us each morning with your unfailing love,
  so we may sing for joy to the end of our lives.
¹⁵ Give us gladness in proportion to our former misery!
  Replace the evil years with good.
¹⁶ Let us, your servants, see you work again;
  let our children see your glory.
¹⁷ And may the Lord our God show us his approval
  and make our efforts successful.
  Yes, make our efforts successful!

91 ¹ *Those who live in the shelter of the Most High*

  will find rest in the shadow of the Almighty.

² This I declare about the Lord:
  He alone is my refuge, my place of safety;
  he is my God, and I trust him.
³ For he will rescue you from every trap
  and protect you from deadly disease.

  ⁴ *He will cover you with his feathers. He will*
shelter you with his wings. His faithful promises
are your armor and protection.

⁵ Do not be afraid of the terrors of the night,
  nor the arrow that flies in the day.

For he will ORDER HIS ANGELS to protect you wherever you go.

Psalm 91:11

⁶ Do not dread the disease that stalks in darkness,
   nor the disaster that strikes at midday.
⁷ Though a thousand fall at your side,
   though ten thousand are dying around you,
   these evils will not touch you.
⁸ Just open your eyes,
   and see how the wicked are punished.

⁹ *If you make the Lord your refuge,*

   if you make the Most High your shelter,

¹⁰ no evil will conquer you;
   no plague will come near your home.

¹¹ *For he will order his angels*
   to protect you wherever you go.

¹² They will hold you up with their hands
   so you won't even hurt your foot on a stone.
¹³ You will trample upon lions and cobras;
   you will crush fierce lions and serpents under
      your feet!

¹⁴ The Lord says, "I will rescue those who love me.
   I will protect those who trust in my name.
¹⁵ When they call on me, I will answer;
   I will be with them in trouble.
   I will rescue and honor them.
¹⁶ I will reward them with a long life
   and give them my salvation."

92 *A psalm. A song to be sung on the Sabbath Day.*

¹ It is good to give thanks to the Lord,
   to sing praises to the Most High.
² *It is good to proclaim your unfailing love*

in the morning, your faithfulness in the evening,

³ accompanied by a ten-stringed instrument, a harp,
   and the melody of a lyre.

⁴ You thrill me, Lord, with all you have done for me!
   I sing for joy because of what you have done.
⁵ O Lord, what great works you do!
   And how deep are your thoughts.
⁶ Only a simpleton would not know,
   and only a fool would not understand this:

7 Though the wicked sprout like weeds
and evildoers flourish,
they will be destroyed forever.

8 But you, O LORD, will be exalted forever.
9 Your enemies, LORD, will surely perish;
all evildoers will be scattered.
10 But you have made me as strong as a wild ox.
You have anointed me with the finest oil.
11 My eyes have seen the downfall of my enemies;
my ears have heard the defeat of my wicked opponents.
12 But the godly will flourish like palm trees
and grow strong like the cedars of Lebanon.
13 For they are transplanted to the LORD's own house.
They flourish in the courts of our God.
14 Even in old age they will still produce fruit;
they will remain vital and green.

15 They will declare, "The Lord is just!
He is my rock! There is no evil in him!"

93 1 The LORD is king! He is robed in majesty.
Indeed, the LORD is robed in majesty and armed with
strength.
The world stands firm
and cannot be shaken.

2 Your throne, O LORD, has stood from time immemorial.
You yourself are from the everlasting past.
3 The floods have risen up, O LORD.
The floods have roared like thunder;
the floods have lifted their pounding waves.
4 But mightier than the violent raging of the seas,
mightier than the breakers on the shore—
the LORD above is mightier than these!
5 Your royal laws cannot be changed.
Your reign, O LORD, is holy forever and ever.

94 1 O LORD, the God of vengeance,
O God of vengeance, let your glorious justice shine forth!
2 Arise, O Judge of the earth.
Give the proud what they deserve.
3 How long, O LORD?
How long will the wicked be allowed to gloat?
4 How long will they speak with arrogance?
How long will these evil people boast?
5 They crush your people, LORD,
hurting those you claim as your own.

⁶ They kill widows and foreigners
    and murder orphans.
⁷ "The Lᴏʀᴅ isn't looking," they say,
    "and besides, the God of Israel doesn't care."

⁸ Think again, you fools!
    When will you finally catch on?
⁹ Is he deaf—the one who made your ears?
    Is he blind—the one who formed your eyes?
¹⁰ He punishes the nations—won't he also punish you?
    He knows everything—doesn't he also know what you are doing?
¹¹ The Lᴏʀᴅ knows people's thoughts;
    he knows they are worthless!

¹² Joyful are those you discipline, Lᴏʀᴅ,
    those you teach with your instructions.
¹³ You give them relief from troubled times
    until a pit is dug to capture the wicked.

¹⁴ *The Lord* will not reject *his people;*

    he will not abandon his special possession.

¹⁵ Judgment will again be founded on justice,
    and those with virtuous hearts will pursue it.

¹⁶ Who will protect me from the wicked?
    Who will stand up for me against evildoers?
¹⁷ Unless the Lᴏʀᴅ had helped me,
    I would soon have settled in the silence of the grave.
¹⁸ I cried out, "I am slipping!"
    but your unfailing love, O Lᴏʀᴅ, supported me.
¹⁹ When doubts filled my mind,
    your comfort gave me renewed hope and cheer.

²⁰ Can unjust leaders claim that God is on their side—
    leaders whose decrees permit injustice?
²¹ They gang up against the righteous
    and condemn the innocent to death.

²² *But the Lord* is my *fortress;*

    my God is the mighty rock where I hide.

²³ God will turn the sins of evil people back on them.
    He will destroy them for their sins.
    The Lᴏʀᴅ our God will destroy them.

95 ¹ Come, let us sing to the Lᴏʀᴅ!
    Let us shout joyfully to the Rock of our salvation.
² Let us come to him with thanksgiving.
    Let us sing psalms of praise to him.

THE LORD will not reject His PEOPLE

PSALM 94:14

³ For the LORD is a great God,
a great King above all gods.
⁴ He holds in his hands the depths of the earth
and the mightiest mountains.
⁵ The sea belongs to him, for he made it.
His hands formed the dry land, too.

⁶Come, let us *worship and bow down.*

Let us *kneel before* the LORD *our maker,*

⁷   for he is our God.
We are the people he watches over,
the flock under his care.

If only you would listen to his voice today!
⁸ The LORD says, "Don't harden your hearts as Israel did at Meribah,
as they did at Massah in the wilderness.
⁹ For there your ancestors tested and tried my patience,
even though they saw everything I did.
¹⁰ For forty years I was angry with them, and I said,
'They are a people whose hearts turn away from me.
They refuse to do what I tell them.'
¹¹ So in my anger I took an oath:
'They will never enter my place of rest.'"

96¹ Sing a new song to the LORD!
Let the whole earth *sing to the Lord!*

² Sing to the LORD; praise his name.
Each day proclaim the good news that he saves.
³ Publish his glorious deeds among the nations.
Tell everyone about the amazing things he does.
⁴ Great is the LORD! He is most worthy of praise!
He is to be feared above all gods.
⁵ The gods of other nations are mere idols,
but the LORD made the heavens!
⁶*Honor and majesty* surround him;

strength & beauty fill his sanctuary.

⁷ O nations of the world, recognize the LORD;
recognize that the LORD is glorious and strong.
⁸ Give to the LORD the glory he deserves!
Bring your offering and come into his courts.
⁹ Worship the LORD in all his holy splendor.
Let all the earth tremble before him.
¹⁰ Tell all the nations, "The LORD reigns!"
The world stands firm and cannot be shaken.
He will judge all peoples fairly.

¹¹Let the *heavens* be glad,
and the earth *rejoice!* Let the sea
and everything in it *shout his praise!*

¹² Let the fields and their crops burst out with joy!
Let the trees of the forest sing for joy
¹³ before the LORD, for he is coming!
He is coming to judge the earth.
He will judge the world with justice,
and the nations with his truth.

97 ¹ The LORD is king!
Let the earth rejoice!

Let the farthest coastlands be glad.
² Dark clouds surround him.
Righteousness and justice are the foundation of his throne.
³ Fire spreads ahead of him
and burns up all his foes.
⁴ His lightning flashes out across the world.
The earth sees and trembles.
⁵ The mountains melt like wax before the LORD,
before the Lord of all the earth.
⁶ The heavens proclaim his righteousness;
every nation sees his glory.
⁷ Those who worship idols are disgraced—
all who brag about their worthless gods—
for every god must bow to him.
⁸ Jerusalem has heard and rejoiced,
and all the towns of Judah are glad
because of your justice, O LORD!
⁹ *For you,* O LORD, *are supreme* over all

the earth; you are *exalted* far above all gods.

¹⁰ You who love the LORD, hate evil!
He protects the lives of his godly people
and rescues them from the power of the wicked.
¹¹ Light shines on the godly,
and joy on those whose hearts are right.
¹² *May all who are godly rejoice*

in the LORD and *praise his holy name!*

98 *A psalm.*

¹ *Sing a new song* to *the Lord,*
for he has done *wonderful deeds.*
His right hand has won a *mighty victory;*
his holy arm has shown his *saving power!*

² The LORD has announced his victory
and has revealed his righteousness to every nation!
³ He has remembered his promise to love and be faithful to Israel.
The ends of the earth have seen the victory of our God.

⁴ Shout to the LORD, all the earth;
break out in praise and sing for joy!
⁵ Sing your praise to the LORD with the harp,
with the harp and melodious song,
⁶ with trumpets and the sound of the ram's horn.
Make a joyful symphony before the LORD, the King!

⁷ Let the sea and everything in it shout his praise!
Let the earth and all living things join in.
⁸ Let the rivers clap their hands in glee!
Let the hills sing out their songs of joy
⁹ before the LORD,
for he is coming to judge the earth.
He will judge the world with justice,
and the nations with fairness.

99 ¹ The LORD is king!
Let the nations tremble!
He sits on his throne between the cherubim.
Let the whole earth quake!
² The LORD sits in majesty in Jerusalem,
exalted above all the nations.
³ Let them praise your great and awesome name.
Your name is holy!
⁴ Mighty King, lover of justice,
you have established fairness.
You have acted with justice
and righteousness throughout Israel.

⁵ *Exalt* the LORD our God!
Bow low before his feet, for he is *holy!*

⁶ Moses and Aaron were among his priests;
Samuel also called on his name.
They cried to the LORD for help,
and he answered them.

⁷ He spoke to Israel from the pillar of cloud,
  and they followed the laws and decrees he gave them.
⁸ O Lᴏʀᴅ our God, you answered them.
  You were a forgiving God to them,
  but you punished them when they went wrong.

⁹ Exalt the Lᴏʀᴅ our God,
  and worship at his holy mountain in Jerusalem,
  for the Lᴏʀᴅ our God is holy!

100 *A psalm of thanksgiving.*

¹*Shout with joy to the Lord, all the earth!*

² Worship the Lᴏʀᴅ with gladness.
  Come before him, singing with joy.
³ Acknowledge that the Lᴏʀᴅ is God!
  He made us, and we are his.
  We are his people, the sheep of his pasture.
⁴ Enter his gates with thanksgiving;
  go into his courts with praise.
  Give thanks to him and praise his name.

⁵*For the Lord is good.*

  His unfailing love continues forever,
  and his faithfulness continues to each generation.

101 *A psalm of David.*

¹*I will sing of your love and justice, Lord.*

  I will *praise you with songs.*

² I will be careful to live a blameless life—
  when will you come to help me?
 I will lead a life of integrity
  in my own home.
³ I will refuse to look at
  anything vile and vulgar.
 I hate all who deal crookedly;
  I will have nothing to do with them.
⁴ I will reject perverse ideas
  and stay away from every evil.
⁵ I will not tolerate people who slander their neighbors.
  I will not endure conceit and pride.

For the Lord is Good

PSALM 100:5

LORD, hear my prayer! Listen to my PLEA!

PSALM 102:1

⁶ *I will search for faithful people*

to be my *companions.*

Only those who are above reproach
will be allowed to serve me.
⁷ I will not allow deceivers to serve in my house,
and liars will not stay in my presence.
⁸ My daily task will be to ferret out the wicked
and free the city of the LORD from their grip.

102 *A prayer of one overwhelmed with trouble, pouring out problems before the LORD.*

¹ *Lord,* hear my *prayer!*
Listen to my plea!
² Don't turn away from me
in my time of distress.
Bend down to listen,
and answer me quickly when I call to you.
³ For my days disappear like smoke,
and my bones burn like red-hot coals.
⁴ My heart is sick, withered like grass,
and I have lost my appetite.
⁵ Because of my groaning,
I am reduced to skin and bones.
⁶ I am like an owl in the desert,
like a little owl in a far-off wilderness.
⁷ I lie awake,
lonely as a solitary bird on the roof.
⁸ My enemies taunt me day after day.
They mock and curse me.
⁹ I eat ashes for food.
My tears run down into my drink
¹⁰ because of your anger and wrath.
For you have picked me up and thrown me out.
¹¹ My life passes as swiftly as the evening shadows.
I am withering away like grass.

¹² *But you, O Lord,* will sit on your *throne forever.*
Your fame will endure to every *generation.*

¹³ You will arise and have mercy on Jerusalem—
and now is the time to pity her,
now is the time you promised to help.
¹⁴ For your people love every stone in her walls
and cherish even the dust in her streets.
¹⁵ Then the nations will tremble before the LORD.
The kings of the earth will tremble before his glory.

¹⁶ For the LORD will rebuild Jerusalem.
    He will appear in his glory.
¹⁷ He will listen to the prayers of the destitute.
    He will not reject their pleas.

¹⁸ Let this be recorded for future generations,
    so that a people not yet born will praise the LORD.
¹⁹ Tell them the LORD looked down
    from his heavenly sanctuary.
  He looked down to earth from heaven
²⁰   to hear the groans of the prisoners,
    to release those condemned to die.
²¹ And so the LORD's fame will be celebrated in Zion,
    his praises in Jerusalem,
²² when multitudes gather together
    and kingdoms come to worship the LORD.

²³ He broke my strength in midlife,
    cutting short my days.
²⁴ But I cried to him, "O my God, who lives forever,
    don't take my life while I am so young!
²⁵ Long ago you laid the foundation of the earth
    and made the heavens with your hands.
²⁶ They will perish, but you remain forever;
    they will wear out like old clothing.
  You will change them like a garment
    and discard them.
²⁷ *But you are* always the same;
    you will *live forever.*

²⁸ The children of your people
    will live in security.
  Their children's children
    will thrive in your presence."

103 *A psalm of David.*

¹ Let all that I am praise the LORD;
    with my whole heart, I will praise his holy name.
² Let all that I am praise the LORD;
    may I never forget the good things he does for me.
³ *He forgives* all my sins
    and *heals* all my diseases.
⁴ He redeems me from death
    and crowns me with love and tender mercies.
⁵ He fills my life with good things.
    My youth is renewed like the eagle's!

⁶ The LORD gives righteousness
 and justice to all who are treated unfairly.

⁷ He revealed his character to Moses
 and his deeds to the people of Israel.

⁸ *The Lord is compassionate and merciful,*

slow to get angry and filled with unfailing love.

⁹ He will not constantly accuse us,
 nor remain angry forever.

¹⁰ He does not punish us for all our sins;
 he does not deal harshly with us, as we deserve.

¹¹ For his unfailing love toward those who fear him
 is as great as the height of the heavens above the earth.

¹² He has removed our sins as far from us
 as the east is from the west.

¹³ *The Lord is like a father to his children,*
 tender and compassionate to those who fear him.

¹⁴ For he knows how weak we are;
 he remembers we are only dust.

¹⁵ Our days on earth are like grass;
 like wildflowers, we bloom and die.

¹⁶ The wind blows, and we are gone—
 as though we had never been here.

¹⁷ But the love of the LORD remains forever
 with those who fear him.

His salvation extends to the children's children

¹⁸ of those who are faithful to his covenant,
 of those who obey his commandments!

¹⁹ The LORD has made the heavens his throne;
 from there he rules over everything.

²⁰ Praise the LORD, you angels,
 you mighty ones who carry out his plans,
 listening for each of his commands.

²¹ Yes, praise the LORD, you armies of angels
 who serve him and do his will!

²² Praise the LORD, everything he has created,
 everything in all his kingdom.

Let all that *I am praise the Lord.*

You made the moon to mark the Seasons, and the Sun knows when to set

PSALM 104:19

104 [1] Let all that I am praise the LORD.

O Lord my God, how great you are!

You are robed with honor and majesty.
[2] You are dressed in a robe of light.
You stretch out the starry curtain of the heavens;
[3] you lay out the rafters of your home in the rain clouds.
You make the clouds your chariot;
you ride upon the wings of the wind.
[4] The winds are your messengers;
flames of fire are your servants.

[5] You placed the world on its foundation
so it would never be moved.
[6] You clothed the earth with floods of water,
water that covered even the mountains.
[7] At your command, the water fled;
at the sound of your thunder, it hurried away.
[8] Mountains rose and valleys sank
to the levels you decreed.
[9] Then you set a firm boundary for the seas,
so they would never again cover the earth.

[10] You make springs pour water into the ravines,
so streams gush down from the mountains.
[11] They provide water for all the animals,
and the wild donkeys quench their thirst.
[12] The birds nest beside the streams
and sing among the branches of the trees.
[13] You send rain on the mountains from your heavenly
home,
and you fill the earth with the fruit of your labor.
[14] You cause grass to grow for the livestock
and plants for people to use.
You allow them to produce food from the earth—
[15] wine to make them glad,
olive oil to soothe their skin,
and bread to give them strength.
[16] The trees of the LORD are well cared for—
the cedars of Lebanon that he planted.
[17] There the birds make their nests,
and the storks make their homes in the cypresses.
[18] High in the mountains live the wild goats,
and the rocks form a refuge for the hyraxes.

[19] *You made the moon to mark the seasons,
and the sun knows when to set.*
[20] You send the darkness, and it becomes night,
when all the forest animals prowl about.

²¹ Then the young lions roar for their prey,
stalking the food provided by God.
²² At dawn they slink back
into their dens to rest.
²³ Then people go off to their work,
where they labor until evening.

²⁴ *O Lord, what a variety of things you have made!*

In wisdom you have made them all.

The earth is full of your creatures.

²⁵ Here is the ocean, vast and wide,
teeming with life of every kind,
both large and small.
²⁶ See the ships sailing along,
and Leviathan, which you made to play in the sea.

²⁷ They all depend on you
to give them food as they need it.
²⁸ When you supply it, they gather it.
You open your hand to feed them,
and they are richly satisfied.
²⁹ But if you turn away from them, they panic.
When you take away their breath,
they die and turn again to dust.
³⁰ When you give them your breath, life is created,
and you renew the face of the earth.

³¹ *May the glory of the Lord continue forever!*

The Lord takes pleasure in all he has made!

³² The earth trembles at his glance;
the mountains smoke at his touch.

³³ I will sing to the LORD as long as I live.
I will praise my God to my last breath!
³⁴ May all my thoughts be pleasing to him,
for I rejoice in the LORD.
³⁵ Let all sinners vanish from the face of the earth;
let the wicked disappear forever.

Let all that I am praise the LORD.

Praise the Lord!

Search for the Lord and for His strength, continually seek him

PSALM 105:4

105 ¹ Give thanks to the LORD and proclaim his greatness.
Let the whole world know what he has done.
² Sing to him; yes, sing his praises.
Tell everyone about his wonderful deeds.
³ Exult in his holy name;
rejoice, you who worship the LORD.

⁴ *Search for the Lord*
and for his strength;
continually seek him.

⁵ Remember the wonders he has performed,
his miracles, and the rulings he has given,
⁶ you children of his servant Abraham,
you descendants of Jacob, his chosen ones.

⁷ He is the LORD our God.
His justice is seen throughout the land.
⁸ He always stands by his covenant—
the commitment he made to a thousand generations.
⁹ This is the covenant he made with Abraham
and the oath he swore to Isaac.
¹⁰ He confirmed it to Jacob as a decree,
and to the people of Israel as a never-ending covenant:
¹¹ "I will give you the land of Canaan
as your special possession."

¹² He said this when they were few in number,
a tiny group of strangers in Canaan.
¹³ They wandered from nation to nation,
from one kingdom to another.
¹⁴ Yet he did not let anyone oppress them.
He warned kings on their behalf:

¹⁵ *"Do not touch my chosen people,*
and do not hurt my prophets."

¹⁶ He called for a famine on the land of Canaan,
cutting off its food supply.
¹⁷ Then he sent someone to Egypt ahead of them—
Joseph, who was sold as a slave.
¹⁸ They bruised his feet with fetters
and placed his neck in an iron collar.

¹⁹ *Until the time came to fulfill his dreams,*
the Lord tested Joseph's character.

²⁰ Then Pharaoh sent for him and set him free;
the ruler of the nation opened his prison door.
²¹ Joseph was put in charge of all the king's household;
he became ruler over all the king's possessions.

²² He could instruct the king's aides as he pleased
    and teach the king's advisers.

²³ Then Israel arrived in Egypt;
    Jacob lived as a foreigner in the land of Ham.
²⁴ And the LORD multiplied the people of Israel
    until they became too mighty for their enemies.
²⁵ Then he turned the Egyptians against the Israelites,
    and they plotted against the LORD's servants.

²⁶ But the LORD sent his servant Moses,
    along with Aaron, whom he had chosen.
²⁷ They performed miraculous signs among the Egyptians,
    and wonders in the land of Ham.
²⁸ The LORD blanketed Egypt in darkness,
    for they had defied his commands to let his people go.
²⁹ He turned their water into blood,
    poisoning all the fish.
³⁰ Then frogs overran the land
    and even invaded the king's bedrooms.
³¹ When the LORD spoke, flies descended on the Egyptians,
    and gnats swarmed across Egypt.
³² He sent them hail instead of rain,
    and lightning flashed over the land.
³³ He ruined their grapevines and fig trees
    and shattered all the trees.
³⁴ He spoke, and hordes of locusts came—
    young locusts beyond number.
³⁵ They ate up everything green in the land,
    destroying all the crops in their fields.
³⁶ Then he killed the oldest son in each Egyptian home,
    the pride and joy of each family.

³⁷ The LORD brought his people out of Egypt, loaded with silver and gold;
    and not one among the tribes of Israel even stumbled.
³⁸ Egypt was glad when they were gone,
    for they feared them greatly.
³⁹ *The Lord spread a cloud above them as a covering*

and gave them a great fire to light the darkness.

⁴⁰ They asked for meat, and he sent them quail;
    he satisfied their hunger with manna—bread from heaven.
⁴¹ He split open a rock, and water gushed out
    to form a river through the dry wasteland.
⁴² For he remembered his sacred promise
    to his servant Abraham.
⁴³ So he brought his people out of Egypt with joy,
    his chosen ones with rejoicing.
⁴⁴ He gave his people the lands of pagan nations,
    and they harvested crops that others had planted.

PSALM 106:1

45 All this happened so they would follow his decrees
and obey his instructions.

Praise the Lord!

106¹ Praise the Lord!

Give thanks to the Lord, for he is good!
His faithful love endures forever.
² Who can list the glorious miracles of the Lord?
Who can ever praise him enough?
³ There is *joy* for those who deal *justly* with others
and always do what is *right.*

⁴ Remember me, Lord, when you show favor to your people;
come near and rescue me.
⁵ Let me share in the prosperity of your chosen ones.
Let me rejoice in the joy of your people;
let me praise you with those who are your heritage.

⁶ Like our ancestors, we have sinned.
We have done wrong! We have acted wickedly!
⁷ Our ancestors in Egypt
were not impressed by the Lord's miraculous deeds.
They soon forgot his many acts of kindness to them.
Instead, they rebelled against him at the Red Sea.
⁸ Even so, *he saved them —*

to defend the *honor* of his name

and to demonstrate his *mighty power.*

⁹ He commanded the Red Sea to dry up.
He led Israel across the sea as if it were a desert.
¹⁰ So he rescued them from their enemies
and redeemed them from their foes.
¹¹ Then the water returned and covered their enemies;
not one of them survived.
¹² Then his people believed his promises.
Then they sang his praise.

¹³ Yet how quickly they forgot what he had done!
They wouldn't wait for his counsel!
¹⁴ In the wilderness their desires ran wild,
testing God's patience in that dry wasteland.
¹⁵ So he gave them what they asked for,
but he sent a plague along with it.
¹⁶ The people in the camp were jealous of Moses
and envious of Aaron, the Lord's holy priest.

¹⁷ Because of this, the earth opened up;
    it swallowed Dathan
    and buried Abiram and the other rebels.
¹⁸ Fire fell upon their followers;
    a flame consumed the wicked.

¹⁹ The people made a calf at Mount Sinai;
    they bowed before an image made of gold.
²⁰ They traded their glorious God
    for a statue of a grass-eating bull.
²¹ They forgot God, their savior,
    who had done such great things in Egypt—
²² such wonderful things in the land of Ham,
    such awesome deeds at the Red Sea.
²³ So he declared he would destroy them.
    But Moses, his chosen one, stepped between the Lord and
      the people.
    He begged him to turn from his anger and not destroy them.

²⁴ The people refused to enter the pleasant land,
    for they wouldn't believe his promise to care for them.
²⁵ Instead, they grumbled in their tents
    and refused to obey the Lord.
²⁶ Therefore, he solemnly swore
    that he would kill them in the wilderness,
²⁷ that he would scatter their descendants among the nations,
    exiling them to distant lands.

²⁸ Then our ancestors joined in the worship of Baal at Peor;
    they even ate sacrifices offered to the dead!
²⁹ They angered the Lord with all these things,
    so a plague broke out among them.
³⁰ But Phinehas had the courage to intervene,
    and the plague was stopped.
³¹ So he has been regarded as a righteous man
    ever since that time.

³² At Meribah, too, they angered the Lord,
    causing Moses serious trouble.
³³ They made Moses angry,
    and he spoke foolishly.

³⁴ Israel failed to destroy the nations in the land,
    as the Lord had commanded them.
³⁵ Instead, they mingled among the pagans
    and adopted their evil customs.
³⁶ They worshiped their idols,
    which led to their downfall.
³⁷ They even sacrificed their sons
    and their daughters to the demons.
³⁸ They shed innocent blood,
    the blood of their sons and daughters.
  By sacrificing them to the idols of Canaan,
    they polluted the land with murder.

³⁹ They defiled themselves by their evil deeds,
  and their love of idols was adultery in the LORD's sight.

⁴⁰ That is why the LORD's anger burned against his people,
  and he abhorred his own special possession.
⁴¹ He handed them over to pagan nations,
  and they were ruled by those who hated them.
⁴² Their enemies crushed them
  and brought them under their cruel power.

⁴³ *Again and again he rescued* them,

  but they chose to rebel against him,
  and they were finally destroyed by their sin.
⁴⁴ Even so, he pitied them in their distress
  and listened to their cries.
⁴⁵ He remembered his covenant with them
  and relented because of his unfailing love.
⁴⁶ He even caused their captors
  to treat them with kindness.

⁴⁷ Save us, O LORD our God!
  Gather us back from among the nations,
so we can thank your holy name
  and rejoice and praise you.

⁴⁸ *Praise the Lord, the God of Israel,
  who lives from everlasting to everlasting!*
Let all the people say, "Amen!"

Praise the LORD!

BOOK FIVE (Psalms 107–150)

107 ¹ Give thanks to the LORD, for he is good!
  His faithful love endures forever.
² Has the LORD redeemed you? Then speak out!
  Tell others he has redeemed you from your enemies.
³ For he has gathered the exiles from many lands,
  from east and west,
  from north and south.

⁴ Some wandered in the wilderness,
  lost and homeless.
⁵ Hungry and thirsty,
  they nearly died.
⁶ "LORD, help!" they cried in their trouble,
  and he rescued them from their distress.
⁷ He led them straight to safety,
  to a city where they could live.

8 Let them praise the LORD for his great love
and for the wonderful things he has done for them.

9 *For he satisfies the thirsty*
and fills the hungry with good things.

10 Some sat in darkness and deepest gloom,
imprisoned in iron chains of misery.
11 They rebelled against the words of God,
scorning the counsel of the Most High.
12 That is why he broke them with hard labor;
they fell, and no one was there to help them.
13 "LORD, help!" they cried in their trouble,
and he saved them from their distress.
14 He led them from the darkness and deepest gloom;
he snapped their chains.
15 Let them praise the LORD for his great love
and for the wonderful things he has done for them.
16 For he broke down their prison gates of bronze;
he cut apart their bars of iron.

17 Some were fools; they rebelled
and suffered for their sins.
18 They couldn't stand the thought of food,
and they were knocking on death's door.

19 *"Lord, help!" they cried in their trouble,*
and he saved them from their distress.

20 He sent out his word and healed them,
snatching them from the door of death.
21 Let them praise the LORD for his great love
and for the wonderful things he has done for them.
22 Let them offer sacrifices of thanksgiving
and sing joyfully about his glorious acts.

23 Some went off to sea in ships,
plying the trade routes of the world.
24 They, too, observed the LORD's power in action,
his impressive works on the deepest seas.
25 He spoke, and the winds rose,
stirring up the waves.
26 Their ships were tossed to the heavens
and plunged again to the depths;
the sailors cringed in terror.
27 They reeled and staggered like drunkards
and were at their wits' end.
28 "LORD, help!" they cried in their trouble,
and he saved them from their distress.
29 He calmed the storm to a whisper
and stilled the waves.

For He
satisfies
the thirsty
and fills
the hungry
with
Good
things

Psalm 107:9

HE changes rivers into deserts, and springs of water into dry, thirsty land

PSALM 107:33

30 What a blessing was that stillness
   as he brought them safely into harbor!
31 Let them praise the LORD for his great love
   and for the wonderful things he has done for them.
32 Let them exalt him publicly before the congregation
   and before the leaders of the nation.

33 He changes rivers into deserts,
   and springs of water into dry, thirsty land.
34 He turns the fruitful land into salty wastelands,
   because of the wickedness of those who live there.
35 But he also turns deserts into pools of water,
   the dry land into springs of water.
36 He brings the hungry to settle there
   and to build their cities.
37 They sow their fields, plant their vineyards,
   and harvest their bumper crops.
38 How he blesses them!
   They raise large families there,
   and their herds of livestock increase.

39 When they decrease in number and become impoverished
   through oppression, trouble, and sorrow,
40 the LORD pours contempt on their princes,
   causing them to wander in trackless wastelands.
41 But he rescues the poor from trouble
   and increases their families like flocks of sheep.
42 The godly will see these things and be glad,
   while the wicked are struck silent.
43 Those who are *wise* will take all this *to heart;*
   they will see in our history
   the faithful *love* of the *Lord.*

108 *A song. A psalm of David.*

1 My heart is confident in you, O God;
   no wonder I can sing your praises with all my heart!
2 Wake up, lyre and harp!
   I will wake the dawn with my song.
3 I will thank you, LORD, among all the people.
   I will sing your praises among the nations.
4 *For your unfailing love* is higher than the *heavens.*
   Your *faithfulness* reaches to the *clouds.*
5 Be exalted, O God, above the highest heavens.
   May your glory shine over all the earth.

6 Now rescue your beloved people.
   Answer and save us by your power.

⁷ God has promised this by his holiness:
  "I will divide up Shechem with joy.
    I will measure out the valley of Succoth.
⁸ Gilead is mine,
    and Manasseh, too.
  Ephraim, my helmet, will produce my warriors,
    and Judah, my scepter, will produce my kings.
⁹ But Moab, my washbasin, will become my servant,
    and I will wipe my feet on Edom
    and shout in triumph over Philistia."

¹⁰ Who will bring me into the fortified city?
    Who will bring me victory over Edom?
¹¹ Have you rejected us, O God?
    Will you no longer march with our armies?
¹² Oh, please help us against our enemies,
    for all human help is useless.
¹³ With God's help we will do mighty things,
    for he will trample down our foes.

109 *For the choir director: A psalm of David.*

¹ *O God,* whom *I praise,*
    don't stand silent and aloof
² while the wicked slander me
    and tell lies about me.
³ They surround me with hateful words
    and fight against me for no reason.
⁴ I love them, but they try to destroy me with accusations
    even as I am praying for them!
⁵ They repay evil for good,
    and hatred for my love.

⁶ They say, "Get an evil person to turn against him.
    Send an accuser to bring him to trial.
⁷ When his case comes up for judgment,
    let him be pronounced guilty.
    Count his prayers as sins.
⁸ Let his years be few;
    let someone else take his position.
⁹ May his children become fatherless,
    and his wife a widow.
¹⁰ May his children wander as beggars
    and be driven from their ruined homes.
¹¹ May creditors seize his entire estate,
    and strangers take all he has earned.
¹² Let no one be kind to him;
    let no one pity his fatherless children.
¹³ May all his offspring die.
    May his family name be blotted out in the next generation.
¹⁴ May the LORD never forget the sins of his fathers;
    may his mother's sins never be erased from the record.

RESCUE {me} because you are so Faithful and Good

Psalm 109:21

¹⁵ May the LORD always remember these sins,
　　and may his name disappear from human memory.
¹⁶ For he refused all kindness to others;
　　he persecuted the poor and needy,
　　and he hounded the brokenhearted to death.
¹⁷ He loved to curse others;
　　now you curse him.
　He never blessed others;
　　now don't you bless him.
¹⁸ Cursing is as natural to him as his clothing,
　　or the water he drinks,
　　or the rich food he eats.
¹⁹ Now may his curses return and cling to him like clothing;
　　may they be tied around him like a belt."

²⁰ May those curses become the LORD's punishment
　　for my accusers who speak evil of me.

²¹ But deal well with me, O Sovereign Lord,
　　for the sake of your own reputation!
Rescue me
　　because you are so faithful and good.

²² For I am poor and needy,
　　and my heart is full of pain.
²³ I am fading like a shadow at dusk;
　　I am brushed off like a locust.
²⁴ My knees are weak from fasting,
　　and I am skin and bones.
²⁵ I am a joke to people everywhere;
　　when they see me, they shake their heads in scorn.

²⁶ Help me, O Lord my God!
　　Save me because of your unfailing love.
²⁷ Let them see that this is your doing,
　　that you yourself have done it, LORD.
²⁸ Then let them curse me if they like,
　　but you will bless me!
　When they attack me, they will be disgraced!
　　But I, your servant, will go right on rejoicing!
²⁹ May my accusers be clothed with disgrace;
　　may their humiliation cover them like a cloak.
³⁰ But I will give repeated thanks to the LORD,
　　praising him to everyone.
³¹ For he stands beside the needy, ready to
　　save them from those who condemn them.

110 *A psalm of David.*

¹ The LORD said to my Lord,
   "Sit in the place of honor at my right hand
 until I humble your enemies,
   making them a footstool under your feet."

² The LORD will extend your powerful kingdom from
      Jerusalem;
   you will rule over your enemies.
³ When you go to war,
   your people will serve you willingly.
 You are arrayed in holy garments,
   and your strength will be renewed each day like the morning dew.

⁴ The LORD has taken an oath and will not break his vow:
   "You are a priest forever in the order of Melchizedek."

⁵ *The Lord stands at your right hand to protect you.*

   He will strike down many kings when his anger erupts.
⁶ He will punish the nations
   and fill their lands with corpses;
   he will shatter heads over the whole earth.
⁷ But he himself will be refreshed from brooks along the way.
   He will be victorious.

111 *¹ Praise the LORD!

 I will thank the LORD with all my heart
   as I meet with his godly people.
² *How amazing are the deeds of the Lord!*

 All who delight in him should ponder them.

³ Everything he does reveals his glory and majesty.
   His righteousness never fails.
⁴ He causes us to remember his wonderful works.
   How gracious and merciful is our LORD!
⁵ He gives food to those who fear him;
   he always remembers his covenant.
⁶ He has shown his great power to his people
   by giving them the lands of other nations.
⁷ All he does is just and good,
   and all his commandments are trustworthy.
⁸ They are forever true,
   to be obeyed faithfully and with integrity.
⁹ He has paid a full ransom for his people.
   He has guaranteed his covenant with them forever.
   What a holy, awe-inspiring name he has!

---

111 This psalm is a Hebrew acrostic poem; after the introductory note of praise, each line begins with a successive letter of the Hebrew alphabet.

Fear of the Lord is the FOUNDATION of True Wisdom

Psalm 111:10

[10]*Fear of* the Lord is the foundation of *true wisdom.*
All who obey his *commandments* will grow in *wisdom.*

Praise him forever!

112 *[1] Praise the Lord!

How joyful are those who fear the Lord
    and delight in obeying his commands.
[2] Their children will be successful everywhere;
    an entire generation of godly people will be blessed.
[3] They themselves will be wealthy,
    and their good deeds will last forever.

[4] *Light shines* in the darkness for *the godly.*
They are generous, *compassionate,*
    and *righteous.*

[5] Good comes to those who lend money generously
    and conduct their business fairly.
[6] Such people will not be overcome by evil.
    Those who are righteous will be long remembered.
[7] They do not fear bad news;
    they confidently trust the Lord to care for them.
[8] They are confident and fearless
    and can face their foes triumphantly.
[9] They share freely and give generously to those in need.
    Their good deeds will be remembered forever.
    They will have influence and honor.
[10] The wicked will see this and be infuriated.
    They will grind their teeth in anger;
    they will slink away, their hopes thwarted.

113 [1] Praise the Lord!

Yes, give praise, O servants of the Lord.
    Praise the name of the Lord!
[2] Blessed be the name of the Lord
    now and forever.
[3] Everywhere—from east to west—
    praise the name of the Lord.

[4] *For the Lord is high above* the nations;

his glory is higher than the *heavens.*

[5] Who can be compared with the Lord our God,
    who is enthroned on high?

112 This psalm is a Hebrew acrostic poem; after the introductory note of praise, each line begins with a successive letter of the Hebrew alphabet.

⁶ He stoops to look down
    on heaven and on earth.
⁷ He lifts the poor from the dust
    and the needy from the garbage dump.
⁸ He sets them among princes,
    even the princes of his own people!
⁹ He gives the childless woman a family,
    making her a happy mother.

Praise the LORD!

114 ¹ When the Israelites escaped from Egypt—
    when the family of Jacob left that foreign land—
² the land of Judah became God's sanctuary,
    and Israel became his kingdom.

³ The Red Sea saw them coming and hurried out of their way!
    The water of the Jordan River turned away.
⁴ The mountains skipped like rams,
    the hills like lambs!
⁵ What's wrong, Red Sea, that made you hurry out of their way?
    What happened, Jordan River, that you turned away?
⁶ Why, mountains, did you skip like rams?
    Why, hills, like lambs?

⁷ Tremble, O earth, at the presence of the Lord,
    at the presence of the God of Jacob.
⁸ *He turned the rock into a pool of water; yes,*
    a spring of water flowed from solid rock.

115 ¹ Not to us, O LORD, not to us,
    but to your name goes all the glory
    for your unfailing love and faithfulness.
² Why let the nations say,
    "Where is their God?"
³ *Our God is in the heavens,*
    and he does as he wishes.
⁴ Their idols are merely things of silver and gold,
    shaped by human hands.
⁵ They have mouths but cannot speak,
    and eyes but cannot see.
⁶ They have ears but cannot hear,
    and noses but cannot smell.
⁷ They have hands but cannot feel,
    and feet but cannot walk,
    and throats but cannot make a sound.
⁸ And those who make idols are just like them,
    as are all who trust in them.

May the
LORD
richly
BLESS
both
you and your
CHILDREN

PSALM 115:14

⁹ O Israel, trust the LORD!
  He is your helper and your shield.
¹⁰ O priests, descendants of Aaron, trust the LORD!
  He is your helper and your shield.
¹¹ All you who *fear* the LORD, *trust the Lord!*
  He is your *helper* and your *shield.*

¹² The LORD remembers us and will bless us.
  He will bless the people of Israel
  and bless the priests, the descendants of Aaron.
¹³ He will bless those who fear the LORD,
  both great and lowly.

¹⁴ May the LORD richly bless
  both you and your children.
¹⁵ May you be blessed by the LORD,
  who made heaven and earth.
¹⁶ The heavens belong to the LORD,
  but he has given the earth to all humanity.
¹⁷ The dead cannot sing praises to the LORD,
  for they have gone into the silence of the grave.
¹⁸ But we can praise the LORD
  both now and forever!

  Praise the LORD!

116 ¹ I love the LORD because he hears my voice
  and my prayer for mercy.
² Because he bends down to listen,
  I will pray as long as I have breath!
³ Death wrapped its ropes around me;
  the terrors of the grave overtook me.
  I saw only trouble and sorrow.
⁴ Then I called on the name of the LORD:
  "Please, LORD, save me!"
⁵ How kind the LORD is! How good he is!
  So merciful, this God of ours!
⁶ The LORD protects those of childlike faith;
  I was facing death, and he saved me.
⁷ Let my soul be at rest again,
  for the LORD has been good to me.
⁸ He has saved me from death,
  my eyes from tears,
  my feet from stumbling.
⁹ And so I walk in the *Lord's presence*
  as I live here on earth!
¹⁰ I believed in you, so I said,
  "I am deeply troubled, LORD."
¹¹ In my anxiety I cried out to you,
  "These people are all liars!"

¹² What can I offer the Lord
    for all he has done for me?
¹³ I will lift up the cup of salvation
    and praise the Lord's name for saving me.
¹⁴ I will keep my promises to the Lord
    in the presence of all his people.

¹⁵ The Lord cares deeply
    when his loved ones die.
¹⁶ O Lord, I am your servant;
    yes, I am your servant, born into your household;
    you have freed me from my chains.
¹⁷ I will offer you a sacrifice of thanksgiving
    and call on the name of the Lord.
¹⁸ I will fulfill my vows to the Lord
    in the presence of all his people—
¹⁹ in the house of the Lord
    in the heart of Jerusalem.

Praise the Lord!

117

¹ Praise the Lord, all you nations.
    Praise him, all you people of the earth.

² For his *unfailing love* for us is *powerful;*
    the Lord's faithfulness endures forever.

Praise the Lord!

118

¹ Give thanks to the Lord, for he is good!
    His faithful love endures forever.

² Let all Israel repeat:
    "His faithful love endures forever."
³ Let Aaron's descendants, the priests, repeat:
    "His faithful love endures forever."
⁴ Let all who fear the Lord repeat:
    "His faithful love endures forever."

⁵ In my distress I prayed to the Lord,
    and the Lord answered me and set me free.
⁶ The Lord is for me, so I will have no fear.
    What can mere people do to me?
⁷ Yes, the Lord is for me; he will help me.
    I will look in triumph at those who hate me.

⁸ *It is better to take refuge in the Lord*
    than to trust in people.
⁹ It is better to take refuge in the Lord
    than to trust in princes.

¹⁰ Though hostile nations surrounded me,
　　I destroyed them all with the authority of the LORD.
¹¹ Yes, they surrounded and attacked me,
　　but I destroyed them all with the authority of the LORD.
¹² They swarmed around me like bees;
　　they blazed against me like a crackling fire.
　　But I destroyed them all with the authority of the LORD.
¹³ My enemies did their best to kill me,
　　but the LORD rescued me.
¹⁴ The LORD is my strength and my song;
　　he has given me victory.
¹⁵ Songs of joy and victory are sung in the camp of the godly.
　　The strong right arm of the LORD has done glorious things!
¹⁶ The strong right arm of the LORD is raised in triumph.
　　The strong right arm of the LORD has done glorious things!
¹⁷ I will not die; instead, I will live
　　to tell what the LORD has done.
¹⁸ The LORD has punished me severely,
　　but he did not let me die.

¹⁹ Open for me the gates where the righteous enter,
　　and I will go in and thank the LORD.
²⁰ These gates lead to the presence of the LORD,
　　and the godly enter there.
²¹ I thank you for answering my prayer
　　and giving me victory!

²² The stone that the builders rejected
　　has now become the cornerstone.
²³ This is the LORD's doing,
　　and it is wonderful to see.

²⁴ This is the day *the Lord* has made.
　　We will *rejoice* and be glad in it.

²⁵ Please, LORD, please save us.
　　Please, LORD, please give us success.
²⁶ Bless the one who comes in the name of the LORD.
　　We bless you from the house of the LORD.
²⁷ The LORD is God, shining upon us.
　　Take the sacrifice and bind it with cords on the altar.
²⁸ You are my God, and I will praise you!
　　You are my God, and I will exalt you!

²⁹ Give thanks to the LORD, for he is good!
　　His faithful love endures forever.

Aleph

119

*1 Joyful are people of integrity,
who follow the instructions of the LORD.

2 Joyful are those who obey his laws
and search for him with all their hearts.
3 They do not compromise with evil,
and they walk only in his paths.
4 You have charged us
to keep your commandments carefully.
5 Oh, that my actions would consistently
reflect your decrees!
6 Then I will not be ashamed
when I compare my life with your commands.
7 As I learn your righteous regulations,
I will thank you by living as I should!
8 I will obey your decrees.
Please don't give up on me!

Beth

9 *How can a young person stay pure?*

By obeying your word.

10 I have tried hard to find you—
don't let me wander from your commands.
11 I have hidden your word in my heart,
that I might not sin against you.
12 I praise you, O LORD;
teach me your decrees.
13 I have recited aloud
all the regulations you have given us.
14 I have rejoiced in your laws
as much as in riches.
15 I will study your commandments
and reflect on your ways.
16 I will delight in your decrees
and not forget your word.

Gimel

17 Be good to your servant,
that I may live and obey your word.

18 *Open my eyes* to see
the wonderful truths in your instructions.

19 I am only a foreigner in the land.
Don't hide your commands from me!
20 I am always overwhelmed
with a desire for your regulations.
21 You rebuke the arrogant;
those who wander from your commands are cursed.

119 This psalm is a Hebrew acrostic poem; there are twenty-two stanzas, one for each successive letter of the Hebrew alphabet. Each of the eight verses within each stanza begins with the Hebrew letter named in its heading.

²² Don't let them scorn and insult me,
for I have obeyed your laws.
²³ Even princes sit and speak against me,
but I will meditate on your decrees.
²⁴ Your laws please me;
they give me wise advice.

Daleth

²⁵ I lie in the dust;
revive me by your word.
²⁶ I told you my plans, and you answered.
Now teach me your decrees.
²⁷ Help me understand the meaning of your commandments,
and I will meditate on your wonderful deeds.
²⁸ I weep with sorrow;
encourage me by your word.
²⁹ Keep me from lying to myself;
give me the privilege of knowing your instructions.

³⁰ *I have chosen to be faithful;*

I have determined to live by your regulations.

³¹ I cling to your laws.
Lord, don't let me be put to shame!
³² I will pursue your commands,
for you expand my understanding.

He

³³ *Teach me your decrees, O Lord;*

I will keep them to the end.

³⁴ Give me understanding and I will obey your instructions;
I will put them into practice with all my heart.
³⁵ Make me walk along the path of your commands,
for that is where my happiness is found.
³⁶ Give me an eagerness for your laws
rather than a love for money!
³⁷ Turn my eyes from worthless things,
and give me life through your word.
³⁸ Reassure me of your promise,
made to those who fear you.
³⁹ Help me abandon my shameful ways;
for your regulations are good.
⁴⁰ I long to obey your commandments!
Renew my life with your goodness.

Waw

⁴¹ *Lord, give me your unfailing love,*

the salvation that you promised me.

Remember YOUR promise to me; it is my Only Hope

Psalm 119:49

⁴² Then I can answer those who taunt me,
 for I trust in your word.
⁴³ Do not snatch your word of truth from me,
 for your regulations are my only hope.
⁴⁴ I will keep on obeying your instructions
 forever and ever.
⁴⁵ I will walk in freedom,
 for I have devoted myself to your commandments.
⁴⁶ I will speak to kings about your laws,
 and I will not be ashamed.
⁴⁷ How I delight in your commands!
 How I love them!
⁴⁸ I honor and love your commands.
 I meditate on your decrees.

Zayin

⁴⁹ *Remember your promise to me;*
 it is my only hope.

⁵⁰ Your promise revives me;
 it comforts me in all my troubles.
⁵¹ The proud hold me in utter contempt,
 but I do not turn away from your instructions.
⁵² I meditate on your age-old regulations;
 O Lᴏʀᴅ, they comfort me.
⁵³ I become furious with the wicked,
 because they reject your instructions.
⁵⁴ Your decrees have been the theme of my songs
 wherever I have lived.
⁵⁵ I reflect at night on who you are, O Lᴏʀᴅ;
 therefore, I obey your instructions.
⁵⁶ This is how I spend my life:
 obeying your commandments.

Heth

⁵⁷ *Lord, you are mine!*
 I promise to obey your words!

⁵⁸ With all my heart I want your blessings.
 Be merciful as you promised.
⁵⁹ *I pondered the direction of my life,*
 and I turned to follow your laws.

⁶⁰ I will hurry, without delay,
 to obey your commands.
⁶¹ Evil people try to drag me into sin,
 but I am firmly anchored to your instructions.
⁶² I rise at midnight to thank you
 for your just regulations.

63 I am a friend to anyone who fears you—
　　anyone who obeys your commandments.
64 O LORD, your unfailing love fills the earth;
　　teach me your decrees.

Teth

65 You have done many good things for me, LORD,
　　just as you promised.
66 I believe in your commands;
　　now teach me good judgment and knowledge.
67 I used to wander off until you disciplined me;
　　but now I closely follow your word.
68 You are good and do only good;
　　teach me your decrees.
69 Arrogant people smear me with lies,
　　but in truth I obey your commandments with all my heart.
70 Their hearts are dull and stupid,
　　but I delight in your instructions.
71 My suffering was good for me,
　　for it taught me to pay attention to your decrees.
72 Your instructions are more valuable to me
　　than millions in gold and silver.

Yodh

73 You made me; you created me.
　　Now give me the sense to follow your commands.
74 *May all who fear you find in me a cause for joy,*

for I have put my hope in your word.

75 I know, O LORD, that your regulations are fair;
　　you disciplined me because I needed it.
76 Now let your unfailing love comfort me,
　　just as you promised me, your servant.
77 Surround me with your tender mercies so I may live,
　　for your instructions are my delight.
78 Bring disgrace upon the arrogant people who lied about me;
　　meanwhile, I will concentrate on your commandments.
79 Let me be united with all who fear you,
　　with those who know your laws.
80 May I be blameless in keeping your decrees;
　　then I will never be ashamed.

Kaph

81 I am worn out waiting for your rescue,
　　but I have put my hope in your word.
82 My eyes are straining to see your promises come true.
　　When will you comfort me?
83 I am shriveled like a wineskin in the smoke,
　　but I have not forgotten to obey your decrees.
84 How long must I wait?
　　When will you punish those who persecute me?

How sweet are your words to me; they are sweeter than honey

PSALM 119:103

85 These arrogant people who hate your instructions
have dug deep pits to trap me.
86 All your commands are trustworthy.
Protect me from those who hunt me down without cause.
87 They almost finished me off,
but I refused to abandon your commandments.
88 In your *unfailing love,* spare my life;
then I can continue *to obey your laws.*

Lamedh

89 *Your eternal word, O Lord,*
stands firm in *heaven.*
90 Your faithfulness extends to every generation,
as enduring as the earth you created.
91 Your regulations remain true to this day,
for everything serves your plans.
92 If your instructions hadn't sustained me with joy,
I would have died in my misery.
93 I will never forget your commandments,
for by them you give me life.
94 I am yours; rescue me!
For I have worked hard at obeying your commandments.
95 Though the wicked hide along the way to kill me,
I will quietly keep my mind on your laws.
96 Even *perfection* has its limits,
but *your* **commands** have no limit.

Mem

97 Oh, how I love your instructions!
I think about them all day long.
98 Your commands make me wiser than my enemies,
for they are my constant guide.
99 Yes, I have more insight than my teachers,
for I am always thinking of your laws.
100 I am even wiser than my elders,
for I have kept your commandments.
101 I have refused to walk on any evil path,
so that I may remain obedient to your word.
102 I haven't turned away from your regulations,
for you have taught me well.
103 *How sweet your words taste to me;*
they are sweeter than honey.

104 Your commandments give me understanding;
no wonder I hate every false way of life.

Nun

105 Your word is a lamp to guide my feet
and a light for my path.
106 I've promised it once, and I'll promise it again:
I will obey your righteous regulations.
107 I have suffered much, O LORD;
restore my life again as you promised.
108 LORD, accept my offering of praise,
and teach me your regulations.
109 My life constantly hangs in the balance,
but I will not stop obeying your instructions.
110 The wicked have set their traps for me,
but I will not turn from your commandments.
111 Your laws are my treasure;
they are my heart's delight.
112 I am determined to keep your decrees
to the very end.

Samekh

113 I hate those with divided loyalties,
but I love your instructions.

114 *You are my refuge and my shield;*
your word is my source of hope.

115 Get out of my life, you evil-minded people,
for I intend to obey the commands of my God.
116 LORD, sustain me as you promised, that I may live!

Do not let my hope be crushed.

117 Sustain me, and I will be rescued;
then I will meditate continually on your decrees.
118 But you have rejected all who stray from your decrees.
They are only fooling themselves.
119 You skim off the wicked of the earth like scum;
no wonder I love to obey your laws!
120 I tremble in fear of you;
I stand in awe of your regulations.

Ayin

121 Don't leave me to the mercy of my enemies,
for I have done what is just and right.
122 Please guarantee a blessing for me.
Don't let the arrogant oppress me!
123 My eyes strain to see your rescue,
to see the truth of your promise fulfilled.
124 I am your servant; deal with me in unfailing love,
and teach me your decrees.

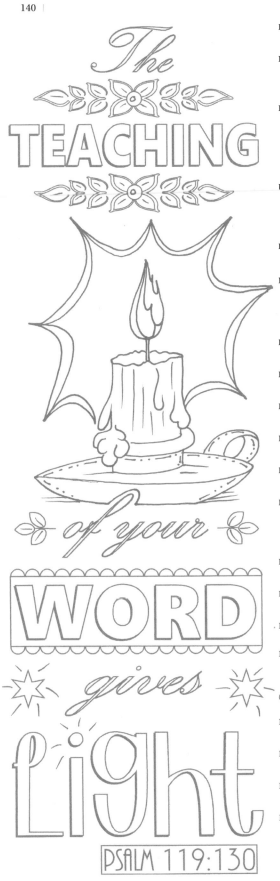

The TEACHING of your WORD gives LIGHT
PSALM 119:130

¹²⁵ Give discernment to me, your servant;
then I will understand your laws.
¹²⁶ LORD, it is time for you to act,
for these evil people have violated your instructions.

¹²⁷ Truly, I love your commands
more than gold, even the finest gold.

¹²⁸ Each of your commandments is right.
That is why I hate every false way.

Pe

¹²⁹ Your laws are wonderful.
No wonder I obey them!
¹³⁰ The teaching of your word gives light,
so even the simple can understand.
¹³¹ I pant with expectation,
longing for your commands.
¹³² Come and show me your mercy,
as you do for all who love your name.
¹³³ Guide my steps by your word,
so I will not be overcome by evil.
¹³⁴ Ransom me from the oppression of evil people;
then I can obey your commandments.
¹³⁵ Look upon me with love;
teach me your decrees.
¹³⁶ Rivers of tears gush from my eyes
because people disobey your instructions.

Tsadhe

¹³⁷ O LORD, you are righteous,
and your regulations are fair.
¹³⁸ Your laws are perfect
and completely trustworthy.
¹³⁹ I am overwhelmed with indignation,
for my enemies have disregarded your words.
¹⁴⁰ Your promises have been thoroughly tested;
that is why I love them so much.
¹⁴¹ I am insignificant and despised,
but I don't forget your commandments.
¹⁴² Your justice is eternal,
and your instructions are perfectly true.
¹⁴³ As pressure and stress bear down on me,
I find joy in your commands.
¹⁴⁴ Your laws are always right;
help me to understand them so I may live.

Qoph

145 I pray with all my heart; answer me, LORD!
I will obey your decrees.
146 I cry out to you; rescue me,
that I may obey your laws.

147 *I rise early,* before the sun is up;
I cry out for help and put my *hope* in your words.

148 I stay awake through the night,
thinking about your promise.
149 In your faithful love, O LORD, hear my cry;
let me be revived by following your
regulations.
150 Lawless people are coming to attack me;
they live far from your instructions.
151 But you are near, O LORD,
and all your commands are true.
152 I have known from my earliest days
that your laws will last forever.

Resh

153 Look upon my suffering and rescue me,
for I have not forgotten your instructions.
154 Argue my case; take my side!
Protect my life as you promised.
155 The wicked are far from rescue,
for they do not bother with your decrees.

156 *Lord, how great is your mercy;*
let me be *revived* by following *your regulations.*

157 Many persecute and trouble me,
yet I have not swerved from your laws.
158 Seeing these traitors makes me sick at heart,
because they care nothing for your word.
159 See how I love your commandments, LORD.
Give back my life because of your unfailing love.
160 The very essence of your words is truth;
all your just regulations will stand forever.

Shin

161 Powerful people harass me without cause,
but my heart trembles only at your word.
162 I rejoice in your word
like one who discovers a great treasure.
163 I hate and abhor all falsehood,
but I love your instructions.
164 I will praise you seven times a day
because all your regulations are just.

165 *Those who love your instructions*
have great peace and do not stumble.

166 I long for your rescue, LORD,
  so I have obeyed your commands.
167 I have obeyed your laws,
  for I love them very much.
168 Yes, I obey your commandments and laws
  because you know everything I do.

Taw

169 O LORD, listen to my cry;
  give me the discerning mind you promised.
170 Listen to my prayer;
  rescue me as you promised.
171 Let praise flow from my lips,
  for you have taught me your decrees.
172 Let my tongue sing about your word,
  for all your commands are right.

173 *Give me a helping hand, for I have*
chosen to follow your commandments.

174 O LORD, I have longed for your rescue,
  and your instructions are my delight.
175 Let me live so I can praise you,
  and may your regulations help me.
176 I have wandered away like a lost sheep;
  come and find me,
    for I have not forgotten your commands.

120 *A song for pilgrims ascending to Jerusalem.*

1 *I took my troubles to the Lord;*
I cried out to him, and he answered my prayer.

2 Rescue me, O LORD, from liars
    and from all deceitful people.
3 O deceptive tongue, what will God do to you?
    How will he increase your punishment?
4 You will be pierced with sharp arrows
    and burned with glowing coals.

5 How I suffer in far-off Meshech.
    It pains me to live in distant Kedar.
6 I am tired of living
    among people who hate peace.
7 I search for peace;
    but when I speak of peace, they want war!

121 *A song for pilgrims ascending to Jerusalem.*

¹ I look up to the mountains—
 does my help come from there?

² My help comes from *the Lord,*
 who made heaven & earth!

³ He will not let you stumble;
 the one who watches over you will not slumber.
⁴ Indeed, he who watches over Israel
 never slumbers or sleeps.

⁵ *The Lord himself* watches over *you!*
 The Lord stands beside you as your protective shade.
⁶ The sun will not harm you by day,
 nor the moon at night.

⁷ *The Lord* keeps you from all harm
 and *watches* over your *life.*

⁸ The Lord keeps watch over you as you come and go,
 both now and forever.

122 *A song for pilgrims ascending to Jerusalem. A psalm of David.*

¹ *I was glad* when they said to me,
 "Let us go to *the house* of the *Lord.*"
² And now here we are,
 standing inside your gates, O Jerusalem.
³ Jerusalem is a well-built city;
 its seamless walls cannot be breached.
⁴ All the tribes of Israel—the Lord's people—
 make their pilgrimage here.
 They come to give thanks to the name of the Lord,
 as the law requires of Israel.
⁵ Here stand the thrones where judgment is given,
 the thrones of the dynasty of David.

⁶ *Pray for peace* in Jerusalem.
 May all who *love this city prosper.*

⁷ O Jerusalem, may there be peace within your walls
 and prosperity in your palaces.

The LORD Himself Watches over You!

PSALM 121:5

THE {LORD} keeps you from all harm and watches over YOUR LIFE.

Psalm 121:7

8 For the sake of my family and friends, I will say,
    "May you have peace."
9 For the sake of the house of the LORD our God,
    I will seek what is best for you, O Jerusalem.

123 *A song for pilgrims ascending to Jerusalem.*

1 *I lift my eyes to you, O God,*
    enthroned in heaven.

2 We keep looking to the LORD our God for his mercy,
    just as servants keep their eyes on their master,
    as a slave girl watches her mistress for the slightest signal.
3 Have mercy on us, LORD, have mercy,
    for we have had our fill of contempt.
4 We have had more than our fill of the scoffing of the proud
    and the contempt of the arrogant.

124 *A song for pilgrims ascending to Jerusalem. A psalm of David.*

1 What if the LORD had not been on our side?
    Let all Israel repeat:
2 What if the LORD had not been on our side
    when people attacked us?
3 They would have swallowed us alive
    in their burning anger.
4 The waters would have engulfed us;
    a torrent would have overwhelmed us.
5 Yes, the raging waters of their fury
    would have overwhelmed our very lives.

6 Praise the LORD,
    who did not let their teeth tear us apart!
7 We escaped like a bird from a hunter's trap.
    The trap is broken, and we are free!

8 *Our help is from the Lord,*
    who made heaven & earth.

125 *A song for pilgrims ascending to Jerusalem.*

1 Those who trust in the LORD are as secure as Mount Zion;
    they will not be defeated but will endure forever.
2 Just as the mountains surround Jerusalem,
    so the LORD surrounds his people, both now and forever.
3 The wicked will not rule the land of the godly,
    for then the godly might be tempted to do wrong.

Yes, the Lord has done AMAZING things for us! What Joy!

Psalm 126:3

⁴ O Lord, do good to those who are good,
whose hearts are in tune with you.

⁵ But banish those who turn to crooked ways, O Lord.
    Take them away with those who do evil.

    May Israel have peace!

126 *A song for pilgrims ascending to Jerusalem.*

¹ When the Lord brought back his exiles to Jerusalem,
    it was like a dream!
² We were filled with laughter,
    and we sang for joy.

    And the other nations said,
    "What amazing things the Lord has done for them."
³ Yes, the Lord has done amazing things for us!
    What joy!

⁴ Restore our fortunes, Lord,
    as streams renew the desert.
⁵ Those who plant in tears
    will harvest with shouts of joy.
⁶ They weep as they go to plant their seed,
    but they sing as they return with the harvest.

127 *A song for pilgrims ascending to Jerusalem.*
A psalm of Solomon.

¹ Unless the Lord builds a house,
    the work of the builders is wasted.
  Unless the Lord protects a city,
    guarding it with sentries will do no good.
² It is useless for you to work so hard
    from early morning until late at night,
  anxiously working for food to eat;
    for God gives rest to his loved ones.

³ Children are a gift from the Lord;
    they are a reward from him.
⁴ Children born to a young man
    are like arrows in a warrior's hands.
⁵ How joyful is the man whose quiver is full of them!
    He will not be put to shame when he confronts his accusers at
      the city gates.

128 *A song for pilgrims ascending to Jerusalem.*

¹ *How joyful* are those who fear *the Lord* ~
all who *follow his ways!*

² You will enjoy the fruit of your labor.
How joyful and prosperous you will be!
³ Your wife will be like a fruitful grapevine,
flourishing within your home.
Your children will be like vigorous young olive trees
as they sit around your table.

⁴ That is the *Lord's blessing*
for those who fear him.

⁵ May the Lord continually bless you from Zion.
May you see Jerusalem prosper as long as you live.
⁶ May you live to enjoy your grandchildren.
May Israel have peace!

129 *A song for pilgrims ascending to Jerusalem.*

¹ From my earliest youth my enemies have persecuted me.
Let all Israel repeat this:
² From my earliest youth my enemies have persecuted me,
but they have never defeated me.
³ My back is covered with cuts,
as if a farmer had plowed long furrows.
⁴ But the Lord is good;
he has cut me free from the ropes of the ungodly.

⁵ May all who hate Jerusalem
be turned back in shameful defeat.
⁶ May they be as useless as grass on a rooftop,
turning yellow when only half grown,
⁷ ignored by the harvester,
despised by the binder.
⁸ And may those who pass by
refuse to give them this blessing:
"The Lord bless you;
we bless you in the Lord's name."

130 *A song for pilgrims ascending to Jerusalem.*

¹ From the depths of despair, O Lord,
I call for your help.
² Hear my cry, O Lord.
Pay attention to my prayer.

O Israel, Hope in the Lord, for with the Lord there is Unfailing Love

Psalm 130:7

³ LORD, if you kept a record of our sins,
who, O Lord, could ever survive?
⁴ But you offer *forgiveness,*
that we might *learn* to fear you.

⁵ I am counting on the LORD;
yes, I am counting on him.
I have put my hope in his word.
⁶ I long for the Lord
more than sentries long for the dawn,
yes, more than sentries long for the dawn.

⁷ O Israel, hope in the LORD;
for with the LORD there is unfailing love.
His redemption overflows.
⁸ He himself will redeem Israel
from every kind of sin.

131 *A song for pilgrims ascending to Jerusalem. A psalm of David.*

¹ LORD, my heart is not proud;
my eyes are not haughty.
I don't concern myself with matters too great
or too awesome for me to grasp.

² Instead, I have *calmed* and *quieted myself,*
like a weaned child who no longer cries for its
mother's milk.
Yes, like a weaned child is my soul within me.

³ O Israel, put your hope in the LORD—
now and always.

132 *A song for pilgrims ascending to Jerusalem.*

¹ LORD, remember David
and all that he suffered.
² He made a solemn promise to the LORD.
He vowed to the Mighty One of Israel,
³ "I will not go home;
I will not let myself rest.
⁴ I will not let my eyes sleep
nor close my eyelids in slumber
⁵ until I find a place to build a house for the LORD,
a sanctuary for the Mighty One of Israel."

⁶ We heard that the Ark was in Ephrathah;
then we found it in the distant countryside of Jaar.

7 Let us go to the sanctuary of the LORD;
  let us worship at the footstool of his throne.

8 *Arise, O Lord,* and enter your *resting place,*
  along with the Ark, the symbol of your power.
9 May your priests be clothed in godliness;
  may your loyal servants sing for joy.
10 For the sake of your servant David,
  do not reject the king you have anointed.
11 The LORD swore an oath to David
  with a promise he will never take back:
  "I will place one of your descendants
    on your throne.
12 If your descendants obey the terms of my covenant
    and the laws that I teach them,
  then your royal line
    will continue forever and ever."

13 For the LORD has chosen Jerusalem;
  he has desired it for his home.
14 "This is my resting place forever," he said.

"*I will live here,* for this is the *home I desired.*
15 I will bless this city and make it prosperous;
  I will satisfy its poor with food.
16 I will clothe its priests with godliness;
  its faithful servants will sing for joy.
17 Here I will increase the power of David;
  my anointed one will be a light for my people.
18 I will clothe his enemies with shame,
  but he will be a glorious king."

133 *A song for pilgrims ascending to Jerusalem. A psalm of David.*

1 How *wonderful & pleasant* it is

when brothers *live together* in *harmony!*
2 For harmony is as precious as the anointing oil
    that was poured over Aaron's head,
    that ran down his beard
    and onto the border of his robe.
3 Harmony is as refreshing as the dew from Mount Hermon
    that falls on the mountains of Zion.
  And there the LORD has pronounced his blessing,
    even life everlasting.

134 *A song for pilgrims ascending to Jerusalem.*

1 Oh, praise the LORD, all you servants of the LORD,
  you who serve at night in the house of the LORD.

Lift your hands toward the sanctuary, and praise the Lord.

Psalm 134:2

²Lift your hands toward the sanctuary,
and praise the Lord.

³ May the LORD, who made heaven and earth,
bless you from Jerusalem.

135 ¹ Praise the LORD!

Praise the name of the LORD!
Praise him, you who serve the LORD,
² you who serve in the house of the LORD,
in the courts of the house of our God.

³ Praise the LORD, for the LORD is good;
celebrate his lovely name with music.
⁴ For the LORD has chosen Jacob for himself,
Israel for his own special treasure.

⁵ I know the greatness of the LORD—
that our Lord is greater than any other god.
⁶ The Lord does whatever pleases him
throughout all heaven and earth,
and on the seas and in their depths.
⁷ He causes the clouds to rise over the whole earth.
He sends the lightning with the rain
and releases the wind from his storehouses.

⁸ He destroyed the firstborn in each Egyptian home,
both people and animals.
⁹ He performed miraculous signs and wonders in Egypt
against Pharaoh and all his people.
¹⁰ He struck down great nations
and slaughtered mighty kings—
¹¹ Sihon king of the Amorites,
Og king of Bashan,
and all the kings of Canaan.
¹² He gave their land as an inheritance,
a special possession to his people Israel.

¹³ Your name, O LORD, endures forever;
your fame, O LORD, is known to every generation.
¹⁴ For the LORD will give justice to his people
and have compassion on his servants.

¹⁵ The idols of the nations are merely things of silver and gold,
shaped by human hands.

¹⁶ They have mouths but cannot speak,
  and eyes but cannot see.
¹⁷ They have ears but cannot hear,
  and mouths but cannot breathe.
¹⁸ And those who make idols are just like them,
  as are all who trust in them.

¹⁹ O Israel, praise the L ORD!
  O priests—descendants of Aaron—praise
    the L ORD!
²⁰ O Levites, praise the L ORD!
  All you who fear the L ORD, praise the L ORD!
²¹ The L ORD be praised from Zion,
  for he lives here in Jerusalem.

  Praise the L ORD!

136 ¹ *Give thanks* to the *Lord,* for he is *good!*
  His faithful love endures forever.
² Give thanks to the God of gods.
  His faithful love endures forever.
³ Give thanks to the Lord of lords.
  His faithful love endures forever.

⁴ Give thanks to him who alone does mighty miracles.
  His faithful love endures forever.
⁵ Give thanks to him who made the heavens so skillfully.
  His faithful love endures forever.
⁶ Give thanks to him who placed the earth among the waters.
  His faithful love endures forever.
⁷ Give thanks to him who made the heavenly lights—
  His faithful love endures forever.
⁸ the sun to rule the day,
  His faithful love endures forever.
⁹ and the moon and stars to rule the night.
  His faithful love endures forever.

¹⁰ Give thanks to him who killed the firstborn of Egypt.
  His faithful love endures forever.
¹¹ He brought Israel out of Egypt.
  His faithful love endures forever.
¹² He acted with a strong hand and powerful arm.
  His faithful love endures forever.
¹³ Give thanks to him who parted the Red Sea.
  His faithful love endures forever.
¹⁴ He led Israel safely through,
  His faithful love endures forever.
¹⁵ but he hurled Pharaoh and his army into the Red Sea.
  His faithful love endures forever.
¹⁶ Give thanks to him who led his people through the wilderness.
  His faithful love endures forever.

¹⁷ Give thanks to him who struck down mighty kings.
  His faithful love endures forever.

¹⁸ He killed powerful kings—
> *His faithful love endures forever.*
¹⁹ Sihon king of the Amorites,
> *His faithful love endures forever.*
²⁰ and Og king of Bashan.
> *His faithful love endures forever.*
²¹ God gave the land of these kings as an inheritance—
> *His faithful love endures forever.*
²² a special possession to his servant Israel.
> *His faithful love endures forever.*

²³ He remembered us in our weakness.
> *His faithful love endures forever.*
²⁴ He saved us from our enemies.
> *His faithful love endures forever.*
²⁵ He gives food to every living thing.
> *His faithful love endures forever.*

²⁶ *Give thanks* to the *God of heaven.*

> *His faithful love endures forever.*

137 ¹ Beside the rivers of Babylon, we sat and wept
as we thought of Jerusalem.
² We put away our harps,
hanging them on the branches of poplar trees.
³ For our captors demanded a song from us.
Our tormentors insisted on a joyful hymn:
"Sing us one of those songs of Jerusalem!"
⁴ But how can we sing the songs of the LORD
while in a pagan land?

⁵ If I forget you, O Jerusalem,
let my right hand forget how to play the harp.
⁶ May my tongue stick to the roof of my mouth
if I fail to remember you,
if I don't make Jerusalem my greatest joy.

⁷ O LORD, remember what the Edomites did
on the day the armies of Babylon captured Jerusalem.
"Destroy it!" they yelled.
"Level it to the ground!"
⁸ O Babylon, you will be destroyed.
Happy is the one who pays you back
for what you have done to us.
⁹ Happy is the one who takes your babies
and smashes them against the rocks!

138 *A psalm of David.*

¹ I give you thanks, O LORD, with all my heart;
I will sing your praises before the gods.

² I bow before your holy Temple as I worship.

I praise your name for your *unfailing love*
and faithfulness; for your *promises* are backed
by all the *honor* of your name.

³ As soon as I pray, you answer me;
    you encourage me by giving me strength.

⁴ Every king in all the earth will thank you, LORD,
    for all of them will hear your words.
⁵ Yes, they will sing about the LORD's ways,
    for the glory of the LORD is very great.
⁶ Though the LORD is great, he cares for the humble,
    but he keeps his distance from the proud.

⁷ Though I am surrounded by troubles,
    you will protect me from the anger of my enemies.
  You reach out your hand,
    and the power of your right hand saves me.

⁸ *The Lord* will work out his plans *for my life* –
for your *faithful love, O Lord,* endures forever.

    Don't abandon me, for you made me.

139 *For the choir director: A psalm of David.*

¹ *O Lord,* you have examined *my heart*
    and know *everything about me.*

² You know when I sit down or stand up.
    You know my thoughts even when I'm far away.
³ You see me when I travel
    and when I rest at home.
    You know everything I do.
⁴ You know what I am going to say
    even before I say it, LORD.
⁵ You go before me and follow me.
    You place your hand of blessing on my head.
⁶ Such knowledge is too wonderful for me,
    too great for me to understand!

⁷ I can never escape from your Spirit!
    I can never get away from your presence!
⁸ If I go up to heaven, you are there;
    if I go down to the grave, you are there.

O Lord, you have EXAMINED my heart and know everything about ME
Psalm 139:1

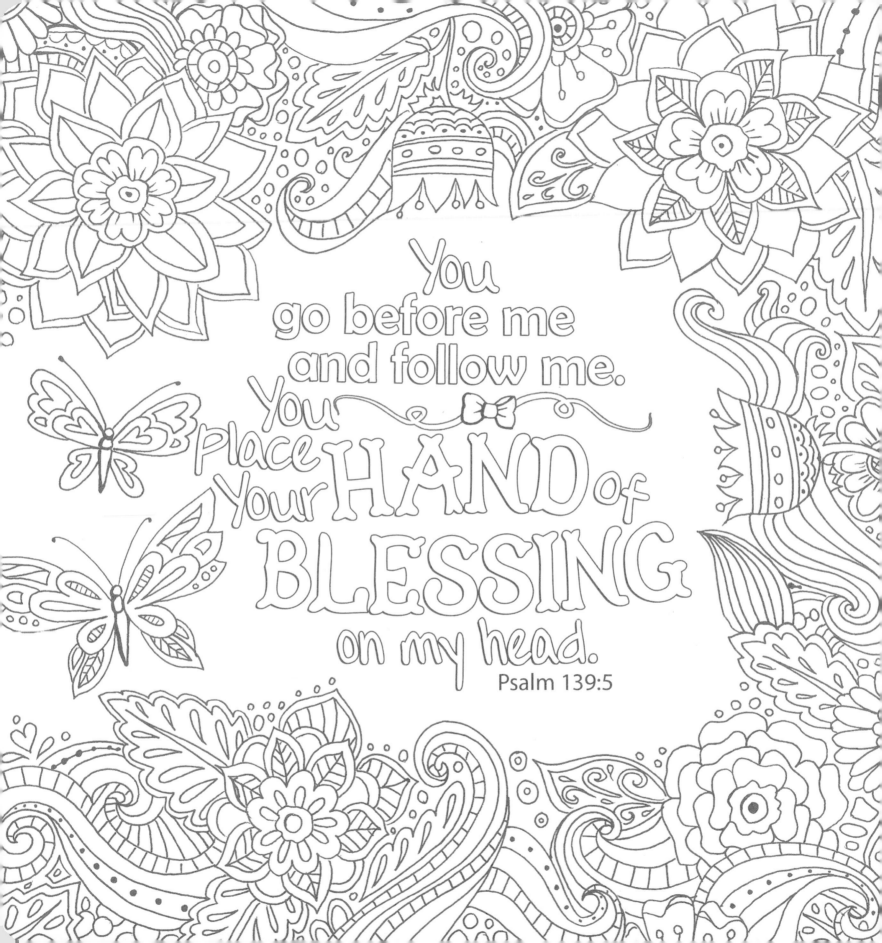

You
go before me
and follow me.
You
place
your HAND of
BLESSING
on my head.
Psalm 139:5

⁹ If I ride the wings of the morning,
   if I dwell by the farthest oceans,
¹⁰ even there your hand will guide me,
   and your strength will support me.
¹¹ I could ask the darkness to hide me
   and the light around me to become night—
¹²   but even in darkness I cannot hide from you.
   To you the night shines as bright as day.
   Darkness and light are the same to you.

¹³ *You made* all the delicate, inner parts of my body
   and *knit me together* in my mother's womb.

¹⁴ Thank you for making me so wonderfully complex!
   Your workmanship is marvelous—how well I know it.
¹⁵ You watched me as I was being formed in utter
      seclusion,
   as I was woven together in the dark of the womb.
¹⁶ You saw me before I was born.
   Every day of my life was recorded in your book.
   Every moment was laid out
      before a single day had passed.

¹⁷ How precious are your thoughts about me, O God.
   They cannot be numbered!
¹⁸ I can't even count them;
   they outnumber the grains of sand!
   And when I wake up,
      you are still with me!

¹⁹ O God, if only you would destroy the wicked!
   Get out of my life, you murderers!
²⁰ They blaspheme you;
   your enemies misuse your name.
²¹ O Lord, shouldn't I hate those who hate you?
   Shouldn't I despise those who oppose you?
²² Yes, I hate them with total hatred,
   for your enemies are my enemies.

²³ Search me, O God, and know my heart;
   test me and know my anxious thoughts.
²⁴ *Point out* anything in me that offends you,
   and lead me along the path of *everlasting life.*

140 *For the choir director: A psalm of David.*

¹ O Lord, rescue me from evil people.
   Protect me from those who are violent,
² those who plot evil in their hearts
   and stir up trouble all day long.
³ Their tongues sting like a snake;
   the venom of a viper drips from their lips.   *Interlude*

4 O LORD, keep me out of the hands of the wicked.
   Protect me from those who are violent,
      for they are plotting against me.
5 The proud have set a trap to catch me;
   they have stretched out a net;
      they have placed traps all along the way.   *Interlude*

6 I said to the LORD, "You are my God!"
   Listen, O LORD, to my cries for mercy!
7 *O Sovereign* LORD, *the strong one who rescued me,*
   you protected me on the day of battle.

8 LORD, do not let evil people have their way.
   Do not let their evil schemes succeed,
      or they will become proud.   *Interlude*

9 Let my enemies be destroyed
   by the very evil they have planned for me.
10 Let burning coals fall down on their heads.
   Let them be thrown into the fire
      or into watery pits from which they can't escape.
11 Don't let liars prosper here in our land.
   Cause great disasters to fall on the violent.

12 But I know the LORD will help those they persecute;
   he will give justice to the poor.
13 Surely *righteous people* are *praising your name;*
   the godly will live in your *presence.*

141 *A psalm of David.*

1 O LORD, I am calling to you. Please hurry!
   Listen when I cry to you for help!
2 Accept my prayer as incense offered to you,
   and my upraised hands as an evening offering.

3 *Take control of what I say, O Lord,*
   and guard my lips.

4 Don't let me drift toward evil
   or take part in acts of wickedness.
Don't let me share in the delicacies
   of those who do wrong.

5 Let the godly strike me!
   It will be a kindness!
If they correct me, it is soothing medicine.
   Don't let me refuse it.

But I pray constantly
    against the wicked and their deeds.
⁶ When their leaders are thrown down from a cliff,
    the wicked will listen to my words and find them true.
⁷ Like rocks brought up by a plow,
    the bones of the wicked will lie scattered without burial.

⁸ *I look to you* for help, *O Sovereign Lord.*

    You are my refuge; don't let them kill me.
⁹ Keep me from the traps they have set for me,
    from the snares of those who do wrong.
¹⁰ Let the wicked fall into their own nets,
    but let me escape.

142 *A psalm of David, regarding his experience in the cave. A prayer.*

¹ I cry out to the LORD;
    I plead for the LORD's mercy.
² I pour out my complaints before him
    and tell him all my troubles.
³ When I am overwhelmed,
    you alone know the way I should turn.
Wherever I go,
    my enemies have set traps for me.
⁴ I look for someone to come and help me,
    but no one gives me a passing thought!
No one will help me;
    no one cares a bit what happens to me.

⁵ *Then I pray* to you, *O Lord.*

I say, "*You are my place of refuge.*
    You are all I really want in life.

⁶ Hear my cry,
    for I am very low.
Rescue me from my persecutors,
    for they are too strong for me.
⁷ Bring me out of prison
    so I can thank you.
The godly will crowd around me,
    for you are good to me."

Take CONTROL of what I say, O Lord, and GUARD my Lips

Psalm 141:3

Hear my prayer, O Lord; LISTEN to my plea!

Psalm 143:1

143 *A psalm of David.*

¹ Hear my prayer, O Lord;
    listen to my plea!

  Answer me because you are faithful and righteous.
² Don't put your servant on trial,
    for no one is innocent before you.
³ My enemy has chased me.
    He has knocked me to the ground
    and forces me to live in darkness like those in the grave.
⁴ I am losing all hope;
    I am paralyzed with fear.
⁵ I remember the days of old.
    I ponder all your great works
    and think about what you have done.

⁶ I lift my hands to you in prayer.

  I thirst for you as parched land thirsts for rain.   *Interlude*

⁷ Come quickly, Lord, and answer me,
    for my depression deepens.
  Don't turn away from me,
    or I will die.
⁸ Let me hear of your unfailing love each morning,
    for I am trusting you.
  Show me where to walk,
    for I give myself to you.
⁹ Rescue me from my enemies, Lord;
    I run to you to hide me.
¹⁰ Teach me to do your will,
    for you are my God.
  May your gracious Spirit lead me forward
    on a firm footing.
¹¹ For the glory of your name, O Lord, preserve my life.
    Because of your faithfulness, bring me out of this distress.
¹² In your unfailing love, silence all my enemies
    and destroy all my foes,
    for I am your servant.

144 *A psalm of David.*

¹ Praise the Lord, who is my rock.

  He trains my hands for war
    and gives my fingers skill for battle.

² *He is my loving ally and my fortress,*

  my tower of safety, my rescuer.

  He is my shield, and I take refuge in him.

   He makes the nations submit to me.

³ O LORD, what are human beings that you should notice them,
   mere mortals that you should think about them?
⁴ For they are like a breath of air;
   their days are like a passing shadow.

⁵ Open the heavens, LORD, and come down.
   Touch the mountains so they billow smoke.
⁶ Hurl your lightning bolts and scatter your enemies!
   Shoot your arrows and confuse them!
⁷ Reach down from heaven and rescue me;
   rescue me from deep waters,
   from the power of my enemies.
⁸ Their mouths are full of lies;
   they swear to tell the truth, but they lie instead.

⁹ *I will sing a new song to you, O God!*

  I will sing your praises

   with a ten-stringed harp.

¹⁰ For you grant victory to kings!
   You rescued your servant David from the fatal sword.
¹¹ Save me!
   Rescue me from the power of my enemies.
  Their mouths are full of lies;
   they swear to tell the truth, but they lie instead.

¹² May our sons flourish in their youth
   like well-nurtured plants.
  May our daughters be like graceful pillars,
   carved to beautify a palace.
¹³ May our barns be filled
   with crops of every kind.
  May the flocks in our fields multiply by the thousands,
   even tens of thousands,
¹⁴   and may our oxen be loaded down with produce.
  May there be no enemy breaking through our walls,
   no going into captivity,
   no cries of alarm in our town squares.

¹⁵ *Yes, joyful are those who live like this!*

  Joyful indeed are those whose God is the Lord.

The Lord always keeps HIS Promises, HE IS Gracious in all HE does

Psalm 145:13

145 * *A psalm of praise of David.*

¹I will *exalt you,* my God and King,

and praise your name forever and ever.
² I will praise you every day;
yes, I will praise you forever.

³ *Great* is the LORD! He is most worthy of *praise!*

No one can measure *his greatness.*

⁴ Let each generation tell its children of your mighty acts;
let them proclaim your power.
⁵ I will meditate on your majestic, glorious splendor
and your wonderful miracles.
⁶ Your awe-inspiring deeds will be on every tongue;
I will proclaim your greatness.
⁷ Everyone will share the story of your wonderful goodness;
they will sing with joy about your righteousness.

⁸ The LORD is merciful and compassionate,
slow to get angry and filled with unfailing love.

⁹ *The Lord is good* to everyone.

He showers compassion on all his *creation.*

¹⁰ All of your works will thank you, LORD,
and your faithful followers will praise you.
¹¹ They will speak of the glory of your kingdom;
they will give examples of your power.
¹² They will tell about your mighty deeds
and about the majesty and glory of your reign.
¹³ For your kingdom is an everlasting kingdom.
You rule throughout all generations.

The Lord always keeps his promises;

he is gracious in all he does.

¹⁴ The LORD helps the fallen
and lifts those bent beneath their loads.
¹⁵ The eyes of all look to you in hope;
you give them their food as they need it.
¹⁶ When you open your hand,
you satisfy the hunger and thirst of every living thing.
¹⁷ The LORD is righteous in everything he does;
he is filled with kindness.

145 This psalm is a Hebrew acrostic poem; each verse (including 13b) begins with a successive letter of the Hebrew alphabet.

¹⁸ The LORD is close to all who call on him,
   yes, to all who call on him in truth.
¹⁹ He grants the desires of those who fear him;
   he hears their cries for help and rescues them.
²⁰ *The Lord protects* all those who *love him,*

   but he destroys the wicked.

²¹ I will *praise the Lord,*
      and may everyone on earth
         bless his holy name forever and ever.

146 ¹ Praise the LORD!

   Let all that I am praise the LORD.
²   I will praise the LORD as long as I live.
   I will sing praises to my God with my dying breath.

³ Don't put your confidence in powerful people;
   there is no help for you there.
⁴ When they breathe their last, they return to the earth,
   and all their plans die with them.
⁵ But joyful are those who have the God of Israel as their helper,
   whose hope is in the LORD their God.
⁶ He made heaven and earth,
   the sea, and everything in them.
      He keeps every promise forever.

⁷ He gives justice to the oppressed
   and food to the hungry.
   The LORD frees the prisoners.
⁸   The LORD opens the eyes of the blind.
   The LORD lifts up those who are weighed down.
      The LORD loves the godly.
⁹ The LORD protects the foreigners among us.
   He cares for the orphans and widows,
   but he frustrates the plans of the wicked.

¹⁰ *The Lord will reign forever.*

   He will be your God, O Jerusalem, throughout the generations.

Praise the Lord!

147 ¹ Praise the LORD!

How good to sing praises to our God!
 How delightful and how fitting!
² The LORD is rebuilding Jerusalem
 and bringing the exiles back to Israel.
³ He heals the brokenhearted
 and bandages their wounds.
⁴ He counts the stars
 and calls them all by name.
⁵ How great is our Lord! His power is absolute!
 His understanding is beyond comprehension!

⁶ *The Lord supports the humble,*

 but he brings the wicked down into the dust.

⁷ Sing out your thanks to the LORD;
 sing praises to our God with a harp.
⁸ He covers the heavens with clouds,
 provides rain for the earth,
 and makes the grass grow in mountain pastures.
⁹ He gives food to the wild animals
 and feeds the young ravens when they cry.
¹⁰ He takes no pleasure in the strength of a horse
 or in human might.
¹¹ No, the LORD's delight is in those who fear him,
 those who put their hope in his unfailing love.

¹² Glorify the LORD, O Jerusalem!

Praise your God, O Zion!

¹³ For he has strengthened the bars of your gates
 and blessed your children within your walls.
¹⁴ He sends peace across your nation
 and satisfies your hunger with the finest wheat.
¹⁵ He sends his orders to the world—
 how swiftly his word flies!
¹⁶ He sends the snow like white wool;
 he scatters frost upon the ground like ashes.
¹⁷ He hurls the hail like stones.
 Who can stand against his freezing cold?
¹⁸ Then, at his command, it all melts.
 He sends his winds, and the ice thaws.
¹⁹ He has revealed his words to Jacob,
 his decrees and regulations to Israel.
²⁰ He has not done this for any other nation;
 they do not know his regulations.

Praise the Lord!

148 ¹ Praise the LORD!

Praise the LORD from the heavens!
 Praise him from the skies!
² *Praise him,* all his angels!
 Praise him, all the armies of *heaven!*
³ Praise him, sun and moon!
 Praise him, all you twinkling stars!
⁴ Praise him, skies above!
 Praise him, vapors high above the clouds!
⁵ Let every created thing give praise to the LORD,
 for he issued his command, and they came into being.
⁶ He set them in place forever and ever.
 His decree will never be revoked.

⁷ *Praise the Lord* from the earth,
 you creatures of the ocean depths,
⁸ fire and hail, snow and clouds,
 wind and weather that obey him,
⁹ mountains and all hills,
 fruit trees and all cedars,
¹⁰ wild animals and all livestock,
 small scurrying animals and birds,
¹¹ kings of the earth and all people,
 rulers and judges of the earth,
¹² young men and young women,
 old men and children.

¹³ Let them all *praise* the name of the LORD.

 For his name is very *great;*
 his glory towers over the earth and *heaven!*
¹⁴ He has made his people strong,
 honoring his faithful ones—
 the people of Israel who are close to him.

 Praise the LORD!

149 ¹ Praise the LORD!

Sing to the LORD a new song.
 Sing his praises in the assembly of the faithful.

² O Israel, rejoice in your Maker.
 O people of Jerusalem, exult in your King.
³ Praise his name with dancing,
 accompanied by tambourine and harp.

PSaLM 149:1

⁴ For the LORD *delights* in his people;

he crowns the **humble** with *victory.*

⁵ Let the faithful rejoice that he honors them.
    Let them sing for joy as they lie on their beds.

⁶ Let the praises of God be in their mouths,
    and a sharp sword in their hands—
⁷ to execute vengeance on the nations
    and punishment on the peoples,
⁸ to bind their kings with shackles
    and their leaders with iron chains,
⁹ to execute the judgment written against them.
    This is the glorious privilege of his faithful ones.

Praise the LORD!

150

¹ Praise the LORD!

Praise God in his sanctuary;
    praise him in his *mighty heaven!*

² Praise him for his mighty works;
    praise his unequaled greatness!
³ Praise him with a blast of the ram's horn;
    praise him with the lyre and harp!
⁴ Praise him with the tambourine and dancing;
    praise him with strings and flutes!
⁵ Praise him with a clash of cymbals;
    praise him with loud clanging cymbals.

⁶ *Let everything that breathes*
    sing praises to the Lord!
Praise the Lord!